CW00555125

International Spoken English for Speakers of Other Languages
Teacher's Book 2 Achiever/Communicator

City & Guilds, the UK's leading provider of vocational qualifications, is a global organisation with over 8500 centres in 100 countries. Offering awards at progressive levels across a wide range of industries, City & Guilds enables individuals and organisations all over the world to achieve their educational aims.

You can find out more about our UK and international qualifications on our website **www.cityandguilds.com**

City & Guilds fully supports the principle of equal opportunities, and we are committed to satisfying this principle in all our activities and published material. A copy of our Equal Opportunities Policy statement 'Access to assessment' is available on our website or from Customer Relations.

City & Guilds
1 Giltspur Street
London EC1A 9DD
UK
T +44 (0)20 7294 2468
F +44 (0)20 7294 2400

First published 2004
Reprinted 2007
©2004 The City and Guilds
of London Institute
City & Guilds is a trademark of the
City and Guilds of London Institute

ISBN-13: 978 0 85193 028 2
ISBN-10: 0 85193 028 X

All rights reserved. No part of this publication may be produced or transmitted in any form or by any means, electronic or mechanical, including photocopy, recording, or any information storage and retrieval system, without permission in writing from the publisher.

Every effort has been made to ensure that the information contained in this publication is true and correct at the time of going to press. However, City & Guilds' products and services are subject to continuous development and improvement and the right is reserved to change products and services from time to time. City & Guilds cannot accept liability for loss or damage arising from the use of information in this publication.

Cover and book design by CDT Design Ltd
Implementation by Phil Baines Studio
Illustrations by Jane Smith
Typeset in Congress Sans
Printed in Hong Kong by Paramount
Printing Company Ltd

International Spoken English for Speakers of Other Languages

Teacher's Book 2
Achiever/Communicator

Contents

Part 1 Giving personal information

Units

Part 2 Social situations

Units

Part 3 Exchanging information and opinions

Part 4 Presenting a topic

Introduction to Teacher's Book 2

This teacher's book is part of a new and comprehensive range of support materials created for the updated and revised Spoken ESOL qualification. The ESOL and Spoken ESOL awards are now available across all six levels of the Common European Framework.

City & Guilds Qualifications	Common European Framework
Mastery	C2 Mastery
Expert	C1 Effective Operational Proficiency
Communicator	B2 Vantage
Achiever	B1 Threshold
Access	A2 Waystage
Preliminary	A1 Breakthrough

Support materials for Spoken ESOL include three student books (each of which covers two levels), three teacher's books and a set of three tapes which support the units. The recordings are not intended to be listening comprehension activities as such. They are examples of natural spoken English and serve as models for students to learn and produce in appropriate parts of the Spoken ESOL test.

As authors, our aim has been to create materials that both help students to improve their spoken English and serve as preparation for the Spoken ESOL exam. With years of experience as examiners (and as moderators of examiners), we know exactly what the examiner is listening for in each part of the test and are very happy to share this expertise with you and your students. We hope that this book will make test preparation, and English language learning and teaching in general, more enjoyable and successful.

ESOL and Spoken ESOL scheme handbooks are also available from City & Guilds and will be extremely helpful to all teachers. These complement this teacher's book, explaining the format and features of the tests at the six levels; they also contain the syllabus and lists of topics, functions and grammatical structures for each level. City & Guilds is also producing a guide for interlocutors, designed to prepare interlocutors for all aspects of administering the Spoken ESOL tests. It is also a valuable aid for teachers who are preparing candidates for the tests. A booklet of sample examinations for these qualifications is also in preparation.

Teacher's Book 2 Achiever/Communicator offers guidance for teachers using *Book 2 Achiever/Communicator*. The design of these books is largely the result of what teachers have told us they would like. Looking at the teacher's book, you will see everything your students see in the student book, plus tips and advice for delivering the units. The idea is that you and your students work together towards their success in the Spoken ESOL test, as you help them develop growing competence and confidence in the communicative use of spoken English.

The books have been divided into four parts, mapped to the four parts of the Spoken ESOL test. There is no need to start at the beginning and work through the book to the end. The Spoken ESOL test is a proficiency test, not an achievement test; there is no need to cover all units or to approach them in any particular order. Your students may come from different backgrounds and their abilities and skills may vary. You will probably be using this book in conjunction with other materials, some of which you have created yourself to meet your students' needs. You will no doubt wish to devote more time to certain language skills than to others with particular groups of students, and will want to use the units as you judge best.

The timings and procedures suggested have been trialled in monolingual and multilingual classes of various sizes (thank you to those who have been involved), and they seem to work very effectively. However, they are there for your reference only; please feel free to follow, adapt or abandon them as you see fit. You may be a relatively new teacher of English or you may have many years of experience – in any event, you are in control of your own classroom and are best placed to decide how to use the units. There is no one prescribed teaching method which has to be adopted by teachers using this book, but we have found that the Engage/Study/Activate model described in Jeremy Harmer's *How to Teach English* (Longman, 1998) works particularly well, and have adopted it in structuring much of these books.

Many exercises in this book suggest that the student works with a partner or as part of a group. The Spoken ESOL test does not involve pairs of candidates; the candidate speaks only with an interlocutor. We have included lots of pair and group activities not to replicate the test, but to give students the maximum opportunity to practise the language skills they will need in the test and in real life. The topics and task types are based very closely on those the students are likely to encounter as candidates in the Spoken ESOL test, and the units are designed to encourage students to develop their speaking skills to match the assessment criteria at Achiever and Communicator levels.

The transcripts of the tapes have been integrated into the Teacher's Book for easy reference but are printed in a section at the end of the student book for revision purposes. Additionally, for some of the exercises, we have supplied possible answers (given in red) that appear only in the Teacher's Book. These are intended to aid you, but are not definitive and, in many cases, such as alphabetical lists of cities, numerous additional answers will be provided by your students.

Tips from the examiners
The 'Tips from the examiners' given in the introduction to each part of the student books offer the student advice specific to that part of the test, and we have expanded on this advice in the teachers' introduction to each part. The assessment criteria – effective communication, accuracy, range, pronunciation and fluency – are applied throughout the test. The candidate is assessed both on overall performance (a global mark) and on performance in each of the four parts; nobody passes or fails on the strength of any one assessment criterion. Certain parts of the test naturally invite a greater emphasis on certain of the criteria and the notes relating to each part of the book will advise teachers on ways of helping their students/candidates make the most of the learning opportunities that these books offer.

At the end of this teacher's book, we have included a sample test within the Interlocutor Framework at both the Achiever and Communicator level. These samples will enable you to see the differences between the exams at these two levels. However, the differences will be not only in what candidates do but also in how competently they do it. The student books do not contain the sample tests but do provide the student with descriptions of the exam at each of the two levels covered by the book. The two sample tests included here can be used to give your student the advantage of a mock exam.

Introduction to Student Book 2

The activities in this book give you a chance to practise speaking English. They build on the vocabulary and grammar you already know and help you learn more. The exercises are designed to build your confidence in key areas: effective communication, accuracy, range, pronunciation and fluency.

You will find that the activities in this book give you maximum opportunity to speak with other students – in groups and in pairs. Speaking with other people is what helps you to use English with confidence, and we hope that these activities will be useful for you and will also be fun. The book has written exercises with spaces for you to make notes of your answers or opinions before you discuss these with someone else. There are tapes to help you improve your pronunciation and develop your communication skills.

Many students who use this book will be candidates preparing for the City & Guilds Spoken ESOL test at Achiever or Communicator. These tests give you a chance to show your skills in speaking English and to gain an internationally recognised qualification. The levels of the City & Guilds Spoken ESOL Qualifications, and of the materials in this book, correspond to the Common European Framework.

City & Guilds Qualifications	Common European Framework
Mastery	C2 Mastery
Expert	C1 Effective Operational Proficiency
Communicator	B2 Vantage
Achiever	B1 Threshold
Access	A2 Waystage
Preliminary	A1 Breakthrough

If you are interested in taking the Spoken ESOL test, your teacher can help you to decide which is the best level for you. Together, you can use this book to prepare for the test.

Who's who in the Spoken ESOL test

The **candidate**, that's you, is the focus of the Spoken ESOL test. There are four parts to the test, and the four parts of this book are specially designed to help you practise the skills you need for each part. In the test you will be invited to answer questions about yourself, play out real-life social situations, exchange information and opinions, and give a short talk on a familiar topic.

Your partner in the test is the **interlocutor** (a teacher). The interlocutor is there to run the test and help you do your best at Achiever or Communicator level. He or she does not correct any mistakes or give you marks.

The **examiner** is not there on the day of the Spoken ESOL test. Your test is recorded and sent to an examiner trained to give you marks in the key areas you will practise when you use this book: effective communication, accuracy, range, pronunciation and fluency.

Tips from the examiners

The writers of this book are teachers with years of success in preparing candidates for the City & Guilds exam and are also Spoken ESOL examiners. They are happy to give you and your teacher advice to help you prepare for the test. Before each part of the book you will see 'Tips from the examiners'. You can use the good advice in these sections to prepare for the test with confidence.

Introduction to Part 1

In Part 1 of this book the focus is on giving personal information. The exercises are relevant both in real-life situations and in preparation for the Spoken ESOL test. In Part 1 of the test, the interlocutor will ask candidates about their background, daily experiences, likes and dislikes. Candidates will always know the answers as the questions are about them. What the examiner will be looking for is how freely the candidate is able to speak when giving personal information.

At the Achiever and Communicator levels candidates are expected to demonstrate the ability to give answers with a level of accuracy and degree of expansion appropriate to the questions asked. Single-word responses will not always be adequate to deal with the prompts put by the interlocutor. The candidate is not expected to ask questions in this part of the exam. However, if there is anything that a student does not understand, he or she should ask the interlocutor to repeat or explain.

There is a specific focus on pronunciation in Part 1, and units are geared to the study and practice of individual sounds and the accurate pronunciation of words and phrases.

Familiarity with the English phonemic chart will be invaluable in helping learners to recognise and aim to produce accurate pronunciation. A recording gives examples of these sounds in standard British English. There are also recordings of people giving accurate responses to prompts of the type candidates will meet in the Spoken ESOL test. These recordings will help students develop the relevant language structures and vocabulary to express their own responses.

Both teacher and student will know in advance some of the things required in Part 1 – for example, each candidate will be asked to give the spelling of his or her name. Spoken ESOL candidates are not expected to produce sounds that replicate exactly those produced by native speakers. The essential thing is that utterances are as clear as possible.

While candidates should be able to answer personal questions without much hesitation, it is quite natural to pause for thought. They will sound a lot more fluent if they are familiar with certain words and expressions commonly used to fill silences. You can help them by giving them practice in using such communication strategies.

1

Part 1 Giving personal information

It is important to be able to speak fluently about yourself. This is often essential in real life for study or work, for travel and leisure, for getting to know people who use English. The units that follow are designed to help you build the language skills you need to talk about yourself fluently and confidently.

In Part 1 of the Spoken ESOL test, you will answer questions about yourself. The interlocutor will ask your name (including the spelling of your family name) and questions about familiar things like the place where you live, your job or studies, the people you know, your daily routine and so on. You will always know the answers to the questions because they are about you.

The units in Part 1 give you the chance to practise speaking about the familiar topics that candidates meet in Part 1 of the Spoken English test at Achiever and Communicator levels. There is plenty of opportunity to work with other students to practise the English you already know and produce this with greater accuracy and fluency, to add to your range of grammar and vocabulary, and to focus on the important area of pronunciation.

Tips from the examiners

You may not always understand the question that the interlocutor asks you in Part 1. Don't be afraid to ask the interlocutor to repeat – he or she is there to help you.

You will probably make a few mistakes – that's perfectly natural so don't worry too much about it. Correct yourself if you notice a mistake, but above all don't let it stop you talking.

Some of the questions in Part 1 need only short, simple answers. Later questions in this part of the test offer you the chance to give more detailed answers. At the Achiever and Communicator levels, you should try to answer in as much detail as you can.

1 Sounds interesting

All candidates will be asked to spell their name at the start of Part 1 of the test (and the accurate production of the letters of the alphabet is an essential part of the learner's use of spoken English). This unit sets out to give students the opportunity to practise the English alphabet in a variety of interesting and interactive ways.

Engage the students' interest in using the letters of the alphabet. One possibility is the game of 'Hangman'.

Hangman is a very simple game and is ideal for practising the letters of the alphabet. Choose a word and on the board put dashes to represent the number of letters, eg, _ _ _ _ _ _ _ _ _. The students take it in turns to give you a letter and if the letter is in the word, you write it in the appropriate place. If the letter is not part of the word, the students lose one point. This is traditionally represented as a sketch of a gallows built up bit by bit until all of the points (normally six or seven) allocated have been used up – but a simple points system will serve perfectly well if you prefer. (5–10 mins)

Organise the students into groups and instruct them to talk together about how each of the letters of the alphabet is pronounced. Several sound like actual English words (the example 'T' is given). It is better not to use dictionaries at this stage and there is no need for the teacher to supply the correct pronunciations as these are given in the recordings. (5–10 mins)

1   **How many letters of the alphabet sound exactly like a common English word?**
Work with a partner and write in the word next to the letter that it sounds like (there may be more than one word for some of the letters). We have filled in one example, 'tea' for the letter T, with the phonemic spelling as well.

A	J jay
B bee, be	K
C see, sea	L
D	M
E	N
F	O owe, oh
G 'gee'	P pea
H	Q queue
I I, eye	R are

S		W	
T tea /tiː/		X ex-	
U you		Y why	
V		Z	

Elicit the students' responses and, without at this stage confirming or correcting, record on the board each group's answer, eg

	Group 1	Group 2	Group 3	Group 4	Group 5
A	✓	-	-	✓	-
B	✓	✓	-	✓	-
C	-	✓	✓	✓	-
D	✓	-	-	✓	-

If you wish, you can introduce an element of competition among groups (eg, if you match the answer in the recording, you get 2 points; if you get an answer wrong, you get –1 point; don't know, 0 points). (5–10 mins)

Play the recording and allow students to check their answers (and total their scores if you make the activity a competition). (10 mins)

2   Listen to the recording to check your answers. 📼 1

📼 1

Male voice 'A? No, I can't think of a word.'
Female voice 'B – yes, a "bee", the insect.'
M 'And "to be", of course. And C – yes, there's "to see".'
F   'And the "sea", as in ocean, but D – I can't think of one.'
M 'Nor E.'
F   'F? No.'
M 'G? Well, there's the expression of surprise. Sounds a little American, "gee!".'
F   'H? No, nothing, but "I", as in me.'
M 'Yes, and "eye" that you see with.'
F   'J – there's a bird, a "jay", but K?'
M 'No, nothing with K, or L, or M, or N, I don't think.'
F   'No, but O, like you "owe" me money.'
M 'And P, there's the small green vegetable.'
F   'Q! A line of people waiting for a bus.'
M 'And R, "we are".'
F   'But no S.'
M 'No, but there's "tea", the drink.'
F   'And U, as in "you and me".'
M 'But nothing in the rest of the letters?'
F   'Well, no V or W, but you can say "ex" as in "ex-boyfriend".'
M 'Oh, yes, and you can ask "why" for Y.'
F   'But no Z.'
M 'No. Still we must have found a word for about half the letters, which is pretty good really.'

Focus on the sounds represented in the letters (using phonemic script if your students are familiar with it). Brainstorm! Ask the students to contribute other words which contain sounds identical to the letters of the alphabet (eg, N (en) is not a word in itself, but the sound is present in 'pen', 'entry', 'again' etc. (5–10 mins)

3–2–1

Engage the students' interest in listening to identify the sounds of the letters of the alphabet by setting up the 3–2–1 game. The recording gives information which, in three stages, makes the answer progressively more obvious (see tapescript). The students, in groups or individually, can guess the answer after only one piece of information (3 points if correct) or wait until two pieces of information (2 points if correct) or all three (1 point if correct) have been given. The winner is the student/group with the most points. (5 mins)

Play the recording. Each set of clues uses letters of the alphabet as its main focus. Ask students if they wish to guess for 3 points, 2 points or 1 point for each of the six clues and record answers on the board. (10 mins)

3 **Listen to the recording. You will hear three clues for each answer. You can guess the answer after the first clue (and win 3 points) or you can wait for more information.** 🔲 2

1 Australia
_____ _____ _____ _____

2 Thursday
_____ _____ _____ _____

3 May
_____ _____ _____ _____

4 orange
_____ _____ _____ _____

5 eight
_____ _____ _____ _____

6 n
_____

🔲 2

1

Female voice 'For 3 points, this is a country that begins and ends with the same letter – A. (pause) And for 2 points, it isn't in Europe or Africa, and it has the letters T and I in it. (pause) For 1 point, and this should make it pretty easy, it contains all the vowels except E and O. (pause) In case you still didn't get it, think of kangaroos and koalas.'

2

Male voice 'This day of the week contains the letter S – 3 points if you get it. (pause) Okay, for 2 points it doesn't have the letter E. (pause) If you've been waiting for 1 point, here it is. This day is the only one to have the letter H in it.'

3

F 'And this month of the year has the letter Y in it. Award yourself 3 points if you're right. (pause) But it hasn't got a J – that's for 2 points. (pause) And for 1 point, if I tell you it has 31 days and contains the letter M, you may get the answer.'

4

M 'This colour of the rainbow doesn't have the letter L in it – 3 points for a correct guess. (pause) For 2 points, it starts and ends with a vowel. (pause) Okay, and for an easy 1 point, think of a fruit.'

5

F **'This is a number from one to twenty and, for 3 points, it hasn't got a letter N in it. (pause) And for 2 points, there's no W in it either. (pause) And I'm sure you'll get 1 point if I tell you that the number begins with a vowel.'**

6

M 'And a final one for 3 points. This letter appears in the word "London". (pause) And for 2 points, the letter is in the word "London" twice. (pause) Okay – your last clue for 1 final point, the letter is not only in the word "London", but it's also in the word "England".'

Recapitulate the different sounds as used in the 3–2–1 game in activity 3. Pay particular attention to any sounds your students still find difficult or confusing. (5 mins)

Tell the students it is now their turn to use the letters of the alphabet to play the 3–2–1 game in competition with fellow members of the class. (2–3 mins)

Organise the students into groups and instruct them to devise 3–2–1 clues for the topics suggested in activity 4 (and/or other topics). Monitor, and correct pronunciation if necessary. Prompt if students lack ideas. For example, for 3 points, 'This student's name doesn't have the letters E or I in it'. Then for 2 points, 'His or her name starts and ends with the same vowel'. For 1 point, 'The middle letter is N'.

Encourage the students to make up as many clues as they can – original ideas don't matter, it's practice of the letters and their sounds which counts. (5–10 mins)

4 Work with a partner or in a group. Make your own version of the 3–2–1 game by preparing clues for your classmates. Then read out your clues and see if other students in your class can guess the answers. Possible topics are:

The name of someone in your class

The name of a radio or TV programme

A well-known place in your town or city

Topic 1

Clue 1

Clue 2

Clue 3

Topic 2
Clue 1
Clue 2
Clue 3

Ask each group in turn to give its 3–2–1 clues for the rest of the class to guess the answers. By this stage, the students should be producing the sounds accurately and confidently, but you may need to make discreet corrections by repeating the clues with an emphasis on accurate production of individual sounds.
(Timing will vary according to the number of students in your class, but should be approximately 2 or 3 minutes per group.)

2 Languages

Engage the students' interest in the topic (languages). One way of doing this is to make a recording of different languages or to put up a few phrases on the board or overhead projector. (2–3 mins)

1   How many languages can you speak and how much can you say in each?
Write the languages you can speak in the left column below.
For each language tick either 1 ('I know just a few words'), 2 ('I know a few phrases and the numbers one to ten'), 3 ('I could hold a simple conversation'), 4 ('I can get by fairly well') or 5 ('I'm fluent') to show how much you think you know.

Language	1	2	3	4	5
English					

Look at the ways in which people describe their own language competence. Explain what is meant by 'fluent', 'to get by', etc. in activity 1. (5 mins)

Instruct the students individually to complete the chart in activity 1. (5 mins)

Instruct the students to compare notes with a partner (using the phrases in the 1–5 list in activity 1). (5 mins)

2   How many points did you score for the languages you know?
Compare your answers with your partner.

Engage the students' interest in listening to the recording by explaining that they are going to hear two speakers talking about their language competence, as in the chart students completed for activity 1. (2–3 mins)

Instruct the students to listen to the recording and to note the points scored by the speakers. (Play the recording a second time if required.) (5 mins)

3   Listen to two people discussing the same task.
Does their total come to more than your and your partner's score? 〔◎◎〕 3

〔◎◎〕 3

Male voice 'So, have you got any 5s?'
Female voice 'Yes, Italian. I lived in Naples for three years and I really picked up the language. What about you?'

M   'No 5s, I'm afraid. I gave myself a 4 for Spanish because I spent a bit of time in Argentina and a 3 for Portuguese because I travelled around Brazil for a few months, and I know I can hold a simple conversation.'

F   'I gave myself a 3 for both of those two and also for Polish. I went to Poland a couple of years ago and learnt a little before I went, so I know more than just a few phrases. And that's that for me.'

M   'I gave myself a 2 in Hungarian – the sort of holiday phrases that help you get by – and a couple of 1 point scores: Slovenian and Russian.'

Play the recording again and focus on the language the speakers use, eg 'I can hardly say a word' and 'I'm pretty fluent in everyday situations'. (5–10 mins)

Engage the students' interest in using the alphabet (it may help to refer to Unit 1). Introduce the topic of the wide range of languages – one idea is to use a world map and to set the scene for discussion of the many languages that are spoken. (2–3 mins)

Organise the students into groups and ask them to see how many languages they can think of in 5 minutes. Monitor, and prompt wherever necessary without actually giving the students the answers at this stage. Reassure students that this is not a test of general knowledge. Exactly how many languages there are is a matter of debate and the object of the exercise is to practise agreeing or disagreeing with partners. (5 mins)

4   With your partner, see if you can find a language which begins with each letter of the alphabet – you have one, 'Arabic', as an example. Take 5 minutes to fill in as many languages as you can. You can give more than one language if you wish.

A Arabic	N Nepalese
B Basque	O
C Chinese	P Polish
D Dutch	Q
E English	R Russian
F French	S Spanish
G German	T Turkish
H Hindi	U Urdu
I Italian	V Vietnamese
J Japanese	W Welsh
K Kurdish	X Xhosa
L Lithuanian	Y
M Maltese	Z

Elicit responses from the students and put on the board various contributions. Focus on the common endings '...ish' and '...ese', and on how these are pronounced. Act as referee and award points wherever possible – don't worry if you don't know all the languages spoken in the world, even teachers don't know everything. (5–10 mins)

Explain that the students will hear a recording of two people attempting to match a language to each letter (in random order). Students are going to see if they beat the speakers' score (they probably will, which will be good for motivation). (2–3 mins)

5   We asked two people to find a language for the letters of the alphabet, but we only gave them 5 seconds for each.
Did you and your partner match more letters and languages than the speakers?
Did they mention any languages you didn't?
Listen to the recording. 🔊 4

🔊 4

Female voice 1 'Okay, ready. I'm going to give each of you a letter in turn and you've got 5 seconds to tell me a language that begins with the letter. To make it more interesting, I've mixed up the order of the letters. Are you ready?'
Male voice   'Yes.'
Female voice 2 'I suppose so.'
F1 'Letter E.'
M   (pause) 'Er ... er ... oh, of course, English.'
F1 'Well done. And S.'
F2   'Spanish ... Swahili ... Swedish.'
F1 'Excellent. What about A?'
F2 (pause) 'No, I can't think of one, sorry.'
F1 'W?'
M   'What about Welsh?'
F1 'Yes. The letter G?'
F2 'Easy. German, Greek.'
F1 'Very good. U?'
M   'Urdu.'
F1 'Good. I?'
F2 'Italian.'
F1 'Good. D?'
M   (pause) 'D ... er ... Oh, yes, Dutch, and Danish.'
F1 'Yes. Letter B?'
F2 'Er ... Bulgarian.'
F1 'Yes. Good. P?'
M   'Lots of them: Polish, Portuguese, Punjabi.'
F1 'Very good. H?'
F2 'Hindi, Hungarian.'
F1 'Letter T?'
F2 'Turkish, Thai.'

F1 **'Good. L?'**

M   'L ... there must be one ... no, I can't think.'

F1 **'You could have Latvian, Lithuanian, Luxemburgian.'**

F2 **'Latin.'**

M   'It's easy for you, you've got time to think.'

F1 **'Letter R?'**

F2 **'Russian, Romanian.'**

F1 **'Yes. C?'**

M   'C? Cantonese, Czech ... what about Cockney?'

F1 **'Hmm ... I'll think about the last one. Q?'**

F2 **'Q?' (pause)**

F1 **'Your 5 seconds are up. M?'**

M   'Mandarin, Malay.'

F1 **'Good. F?'**

F2 **'Farsi, French.'**

F1 **'Yes. K?'**

F2 **'K? No, oh yes, Kurdish.'**

F1 **'J?'**

F2 **'Japanese.'**

F1 **'Good. X?'**

M   'X? ... No, sorry.'

F1 **'O?'**

F2 **'O. There must be one. (pause) No, I can't think.'**

F1 **'N?'**

M   'N? N? No, I can't ... Oh yes, Norwegian.'

F1 **'Yes. And finally, V.'**

F2 **'Is there one? I can't think of any?'**

F1 **'Never mind. You got a language to match more than half the letters of the alphabet. That could be a record! Congratulations!'**

Play the recording – repeating each item if you think it would be useful – and ask students to total the teachers' score. (5–10 mins)

Play the recording again. Focus on how the teachers pronounce the various languages (a variety of the English phonemes is naturally used). (5–10 mins)

3 Study

Engage the students' interest in the topic of study. One way to do this is to draw on your own study experiences and to ask students to guess which subjects you were good or bad at when a student (or take in an old school report if you have one). (2–5 mins)

Instruct the students individually to complete the table by putting ticks against subjects under the appropriate heading. (5 mins)

1 **How do you feel about different school subjects?**
   Put a tick (✓) to answer 'yes' to the questions.

School subject	Do/did you like the subject?	Are/were you good at the subject?	Is the subject useful for real life?
Geography			
Mathematics			
Foreign languages			
Your own language			
Sports and games			
History			
Science			
Art			
Other subjects			

Instruct the students to work in pairs to compare answers. (5–10 mins)

2 **Now compare your answers with a partner.**

Ask the students to give you feedback on what their partner told them. Introduce descriptive vocabulary to expand on 'very good' ('excellent', 'outstanding' or 'very weak', 'appalling', etc). (5–10 mins)

Collocations

Introduce this activity by explaining that certain words and phrases just go together naturally and frequently, eg, 'bus' as in 'bus driver/bus stop/bus fare'. Tell the students they are going to look at words which go naturally with 'school'. (2–3 mins)

3 **We asked 100 people to say the first word they thought of that could be paired with 'school'.**
   Discuss with a partner which words are the most likely to follow the word 'school', beginning with the letters below, and together decide what you think the top answers will be.

school b school book, school bus

school d school day, school dinner

school h school holiday

school t school teacher, school tie

school u school uniform

school y school year, school yard

This activity can be made into a motivating game. Ask the pairs to discuss what words they think will be the top choices – the students can offer different answers (1 point if one of them is right), or can try to persuade each other to agree on a joint answer (3 points if correct). Monitor, and encourage students to come up with lots of possible collocations – there is no 'right' or 'wrong' answer. (5–10 mins)

Tell the students they are going to listen to the recording to see if their answers corresponded to those of the speakers. (2–3 mins)

4 **Listen to the recording. Are some of your answers the same as those the speakers give?** 📟 5

📟 5
Female voice 'There were two top answers for the letter B: school book and school bus.'
Male voice 'And also for D – school day and school dinner.'
F **'For H – no surprises. The most popular answer is something most students look forward to during term time: school holiday.'**
M 'I'm surprised by the top answer for T. I would have expected school tie, but it was school teacher.'
F **'Don't worry. A tie is often part of the top answer for the letter U. That was school uniform.'**
M 'And finally, two top answers for Y – school year and the place where you play: school yard.'

Play the recording, pausing after each of the collocations to allow students to check. (5–10 mins)

School days – the happiest days of your life?

Engage the students' interest in this topic. One simple way is to refer back to your own experiences of school. You can pretend to like or dislike it more than you did in reality – some people will have recollections that are happier than others. (2–3 mins)

Instruct the students individually to note down as many things as they can think of that they like(d) and dislike(d) about school life. (5 mins)

5   It is common to say that school days are 'the happiest days of your life', but is it true for you?
    Make notes about the things you like(d) and dislike(d) about your own school days – not just the subjects, but everything about school life.

What I like(d) about school	What I dislike(d) about school

Instruct the students in pairs to compare notes and say who had more things in the 'like' and 'dislike' spaces. (5–10 mins)

6   Now compare your answers with a partner.
    Which of you has the most things under 'like' and 'dislike'?

Tell the students they are going to listen to two people talking about their school days – do the speakers mention the same likes/dislikes as the students? (2–3 mins)

7   Listen to the recording of two people speaking.
    One of them liked school, the other didn't.
    Do they mention the same things as you and/or your partner?
    Do they express their feelings in the same ways as you? 🔊 6

[cassette icon] 6

Female voice **'School days the happiest of your life?! You must be joking! Apart from the friends I made, I don't think there was anything about school that I liked. All the subjects were boring, and maths and science drove me mad. We had to wear a really dull uniform – brown with bits of yellow. School dinners were awful: overcooked vegetables and heavy puddings. I like sports now, but when I was at school I didn't enjoy them at all – especially playing hockey in the pouring rain. Even in the school holidays they gave us homework. The day I *left* school was the happiest day of *my* life.'**

Male voice 'Perhaps I'm a little unusual, but I actually liked school. I was pretty good at most of the subjects and I got on well with all my teachers. What I liked best was the feeling that you didn't have too many problems or responsibilities – everything was provided for you. School days are definitely the happiest of your life. You have your whole future ahead of you, you have all your friends around you ... what could be better?'

Play the recording and allow the students to check which likes/dislikes corresponded to their own. (5 mins)

Play the recording again. Focus on the language used to express strong and less strong feelings: 'I couldn't stand...', 'I didn't particularly like...', etc. (5–10 mins)

4 Daily routine

Travelling to and from work or school

Engage the students' interest in the topic. One way of doing this is to use props (eg, a bus or train ticket representing a daily trip), another is to invite students to guess the things you do at the same time every day. (2–3 mins)

Instruct the students in pairs to describe to each other their daily trip to and from school or work. If the students have identical trips, you can change the focus by asking them to compare their current usual day with one they have had previously, or with the daily trip of a parent or friend. (5–10 mins)

1 **How do you get to school or work and home again?**
   Describe your daily trip to a partner and see in what ways your trips are the same and different. Here are some ideas:

Time of leaving and arriving

Transport you use

Things you do on the way

People you travel with

Tell the students they are going to hear people from different parts of the world talking about their daily journeys.

Instruct the students in pairs to come up with as many ways as possible of getting to and from work every day. You can increase motivation by making this activity a competition – the pair with most right answers wins. (5 mins)

2 **People in different parts of the world have very different daily routines. You are going to hear people describing their daily trip to work or school; each of them uses different forms of transport. Name as many different ways of getting to and from school or work as you can think of.**

Elicit contributions from student pairs and put some of these on the board, correcting structure or vocabulary if necessary, but without making this a particular focus of this stage of the lesson. (5 mins)

Tell the students they are now going to listen and check if they have included the speakers' routines in their suggestions. (2–3 mins)

3   Listen and see how many of your suggestions are included. 〔▭〕 7

〔▭〕 7

Male voice 'My daily trip to and from work is nothing special. I simply go on
          foot because I live only 10 minutes away from my office. If it's raining very
          heavily I might drive, but I normally walk.'

Female voice 1 'You'll never guess how I get to and from work in the winter. I work in
          a hotel in the mountains and the quickest and easiest way to get around is on skis.
          So that's what I do – I ski to and from work.'

Young male voice 'I live quite a long way from school and I use three different
          types of transport every day. First I ride my bike to the station, that's not too
          far, then I get the train into the city. After that, I take a tram and that goes
          right past my school.'

Female voice 2 'My daily trip to work? Nothing very exciting really. I catch a local bus at
          the bottom of the road and then I take the underground. I walk from the underground
          station to work unless I'm late, in which case I take a taxi.'

Ask the students to tell you what they think you like about your daily
journey to and from work – tell them if they're right. Tell the students
they are now going to discuss what the speakers in the recording might
like/dislike about their daily trips. (2–3 mins)

Instruct the students in pairs to discuss what they think the speakers
may say they like and dislike about their daily journeys. Tell the students
to phrase these as indirect speech and see how close they come to
expressing the same feelings as the speakers and in the same ways
(eg, Speaker 1: 'I really love my trip because I see a lot of beautiful
scenery'). (5 mins)

**4   The same people are now going to say what they like and dislike
       most about their daily trip to and from school or work.
       You have heard how they travel.
       What do you think they may like and dislike, and how will they express
       their feelings? Discuss this with a partner.**

Play the recording and allow students to check their answers. (5 mins)

5   Listen and check your answers. 〔▭〕 8

🔊 8

Male voice (same as 🔊 7) 'I like walking. You can take your time and you don't have to depend on buses and trains being on time. I suppose that the one thing I don't like is having to cross busy roads.'

Female voice 1 'The best things are the view and the fact that I get healthy exercise. The only thing I don't like is the time it takes to change clothes: I have to put on my ski suit then change into work things.'

Young male voice 'I like the bike ride, but the rest is boring. I hate it when the train is late or crowded, and I don't like queuing for the tram.'

Female voice 2 'What do I like about the journey? Well, it's usually quick and easy, and I can read the newspaper on the underground. What I don't like is the rush hour – the underground gets much too crowded.'

Focus on the language that the speakers use to describe their journeys. It is a good opportunity to present adverbs of frequency in order of least to most frequent (or vice versa). (5–10 mins)

always
usually/normally
often
sometimes
occasionally
rarely/seldom/hardly ever
never

Play the recording a second time, this time to allow the students to listen for the language that the speakers use to emphasise their likes and dislikes (stress and intonations, intensifiers, etc). (5 mins)

Ask the students to contribute some examples of the ways in which the speakers make their likes and dislikes clear. Put some of these on the board and draw attention to the ways the speakers emphasised the message (eg, with lines to indicate intonation patterns). (5–10 mins)

Are you in a rut?

Introduce the next topic: Are you in a rut? One way is to reflect on how long you personally have been doing the same things at the same time ('I've worn these shoes every school day this term'). Alternatively, produce your regular daily newspaper. (2–3 mins)

Instruct the students individually to complete the questionnaire. (5 mins)

6   **Fill in this questionnaire:**

Do you get up at the same time every weekday and do the same things?

A always

B usually

C not very often

How often do you change your route to and from school or work?

A never

B occasionally

C often

If you go away on holiday, do you go back to somewhere you've been before?

A always

B sometimes

C never

Do you eat the same meal on the same day each week?

A always

B usually

C never

Do you ever read the same book twice or watch the same film more than once?

A frequently

B occasionally

C hardly ever

How often do you change your daily newspaper or radio station?

A never

B sometimes

C fairly often

Instruct the students to work in pairs to compare notes. (5 mins)

7 **Compare your answers with a partner.**

Ask students to report back on the differences and similarities. (5 mins)

Reported speech is a natural focus in this activity. When reporting their partner's statements, the students will need to make structural changes (from 'I usually eat…' to 'He said he usually ate…', or perhaps more current usage, 'He said he usually eats…'). (5–10 mins)

Tell the students they are going to listen to the verdicts on their answers and to learn whether or not they are in a rut. It is often motivating if you also give your own answers so that you are a part of the group in this activity. (2–3 mins)

Play the recording, allowing the students to check their scores and their 'Are you in a rut?' rating. (5 mins)

8 **Now listen to the scoring system – are you in a rut?** 🔲 9

🔲 9

Male voice 'Are you in a rut? Well, if most of your answers are A, you like to do things in an organised way. You are reliable, dependable. Perhaps you are a little predictable, but at least people know what to expect … and we'll never change you now. If most of your answers are B, then you like to vary your daily routine occasionally, making you slightly unpredictable. Do you have mostly C answers? If so, you're a free spirit – you're definitely not stuck in a rut … the problem, perhaps, is that we can't be sure that you'll keep a promise or do the things we expect you to do.'

The 'Are you in a rut?' scoring system gives an opportunity for you to introduce language of agreement and disagreement (ranging from mild 'I don't think that's altogether fair' to strong 'That is absolute nonsense'). If you have joined in the questionnaire and are suitably outraged by your own score – you can model examples of language of disagreement. (5–10 mins)

5 Occupations

Engage the students' interest by introducing the theme of occupations. Bring in, for example, objects related to various occupations, such as a book to represent librarian or bookseller; a newspaper to represent newsagent or journalist. Brainstorm! Ask the students to suggest as many types of occupation as they can and put them on the board. (2–5 mins)

Ask the students to look at the occupations on the board and to say what these people do. Vary the forms used by prompting, eg, 'What does a waiter do?', 'What do waiters do?' (5 mins)

At this level, the students will be familiar with the simple present construction but may benefit from practice of the third person 's'.

Focus on the simple present in negative form. Ask the students to say what people in these occupations don't do, eg, 'A waiter doesn't cut hair' or 'Waiters don't cut hair.' (5 mins)

After checking that the students understand the vocabulary in the statements, instruct the students individually or in groups to correct each statement as in the examples given. (5–10 mins)

1   **Here are some statements about what people's jobs involve, but each of them is false.**
   Can you correct each statement by (A) giving the correct negative form and (B) giving correct information. Here is an example:

A florist makes furniture.

A A florist doesn't make furniture.

B A carpenter makes furniture. A florist sells flowers.

A photographer sells fruit and vegetables.

A

B

Librarians fly aeroplanes.

A

B

An optician repairs cars.

A

B

Teachers sell newspapers and magazines.

A

B

Hairdressers look after hospital patients.

A

B

An architect takes care of people's teeth.

A

B

Journalists make bread.

A

B

A chemist serves food and drink in a restaurant.
A

B

Engage the students' interest in listening to the recording by eliciting at random from members of the class their suggested corrections, eg, 'An optician sells glasses/spectacles' or 'An optician tests your eyes.'

Explain that the students are going to hear people correcting the statements. They check which are the same and which contain differences. (5 mins)

Play the recording and allow the students to check what the speakers said. (5 mins)

2 **Listen to the recording of people's corrections to the statements. Which are exactly the same as yours? If some aren't the same, how are they different?** 📼 10

📼 10
1
Male voice 'A photographer doesn't sell fruit and vegetables. A photographer takes photographs. A greengrocer sells fruit and vegetables.'
2
Female voice 'Librarians don't fly planes. Pilots fly planes. Librarians work in libraries and lend books.'
3
M 'An optician doesn't repair cars. A mechanic repairs cars. An optician tests your eyes and provides glasses and contact lenses.'

4

F 'Teachers don't sell newspapers and magazines. Teachers teach others.
Newsagents sell newspapers and magazines.'

5

M **'Hairdressers don't look after hospital patients. Nurses look after hospital
patients. Hairdressers cut and style hair.'**

6

F 'An architect doesn't take care of people's teeth. An architect designs buildings.
A dentist takes care of people's teeth.'

7

M **'Journalists don't make bread. Journalists write newspaper articles and
report the news. Bakers make bread.'**

8

F 'A chemist doesn't serve food and drink in a restaurant. A waitress or waiter serves
food and drink in a restaurant. A chemist sells medicine.'

Play the tape again, this time to focus on the pronunciation. Draw the
students' attention to the way the third person 's' is produced, eg, /z/
in 'sells' and /s/ in 'takes'. Also draw the students' attention to the way
'do not' and 'does not' are contracted in natural speech to 'don't' and
'doesn't'. (5–10 mins)

Use the statements in activity 1 to allow the students the opportunity to
produce /z/ and /s/ accurately. Monitor, and correct if necessary. (5 mins)

Engage the students' interest in using collocations by explaining that
there are certain words which naturally go together, eg, 'tea' and 'tea
time/teacup/teapot/teaspoon'. (5 mins)

3 We asked 100 people to add another word to each of the words below.
In each case we have recorded the three most popular answers.
There are lots of possibilities, but can you guess what some of the
most popular answers were?
Choose up to three answers for each word connected with occupations.

Word	Top answer	2nd	3rd
business	person	trip	lunch
office	worker	hours	party
bank	holiday	manager	note
job	interview	centre	share
pay	rise	day	rate
shop	shopping	assistant	window

Explain that the students are going to hear the top 3 answers given
when 100 people were asked to say the word that first came to mind
in connection with those in the list in activity 3.

Organise the students into groups and ask them to discuss the words they think are most likely to be associated with those on the list. There is no 'right' or 'wrong' answer; students can draw on their vocabulary and suggest 3 words for each item. (10 mins)

Tell the students there will be a competition and the group with most points will win. The rules are simple: each group chooses 3 words to match each of the items on the list. Each time they get a top answer they get 3 points, a second answer gets 2 points and so on. Repeat that there are many possible combinations and that the winners will be the ones who happen to come closest to the answers given by the sample of people asked – other answers are not 'wrong'. Ask the student groups to say what their 3 suggested words are for each item on the list. (5–10 mins)

Play the recording and allow students to check if they have given the same answers as the people speaking. It may increase motivation if you pause the recording after each of the items and keep a running total. (5 mins)

4   **Listen to the recording and give yourself 3 points for each top answer included in your three answers; 2 points for second and 1 point for third. Maximum possible is 36.** 📼 11

Scores:

20 points +	Amazing	5–9 points	Not bad
15–19 points	Excellent	1–4 points	Better luck next time
10–14 points	Very good	0 points	It's only a game!

📼 11

1

Female voice 'I'll give you the answers in reverse order: third, then second, then the top answer. For business, the third answer was business lunch, the second was business trip, and the top answer was business person – if you said businessman or businesswoman, that's included.'

2

Male voice 'With office, the third answer was office party, the second answer was office hours, the top answer was office worker.'

3

F   'The next word, bank. The third most popular answer was bank note, the second answer was bank manager, and the top answer was the day when most people don't work – bank holiday!'

4

M   'Job. The third answer was job share or job sharing, the second answer was job centre, and the top answer was job interview.'

5

F   'The third answer people gave for the word pay was pay rate, the second answer was pay day, and the top answer was optimistic – pay rise or pay increase.

6

M 'And finally shop: the third answer was shop window, the second was shop assistant
   … the top answer wasn't really a word, it was "ing". Most people said shopping or
   shopping centre – if you got that, well done!

7

F 'So, how many points did you get? 20 or more – that's really amazing, a
   world record! 15 to 19 – excellent, there are so many words connected with
   occupations. 10 to 14 – still very good indeed. Five to nine – well, that's not
   bad at all. One to four points – okay, not outstanding, but don't worry. Better
   luck next time. If you got no points at all – never mind, it's only a game!'

Focus on some of the collocations in the recording and draw the
students' attention to certain language items which have become
natural usage (eg, 'bank clerk', 'bank manager'). It may be helpful to
check what the students suggested and say whether these are
commonly used (eg, 'bank note' is, 'bank coin' isn't). (5–10 mins)

Engage the students' interest in listening to the recording by explaining
that they are going to hear people describing their jobs. Each of the
speakers gives 3 pieces of information and it becomes progressively
clearer what the job is. (2–3 mins)

Organise the students into groups. Play the recording, pausing as
indicated in the 3–2–1 tapescript. (10 mins)

---

5 Here are some people describing jobs they do, jobs they have done
   or jobs they'd like to do. The information gives more clues as it goes
   on. Work with a partner and say what you think the job might be.
   If you guess correctly after the first piece of information, you get
   3 points, then 2, then, after the final clue, 1 point.
   You can repeat your first choice if you think it's right or change
   as you get more information. ⌾ 12

Job	1st answer	2nd	3rd
_____	_____	_____	_____
_____	_____	_____	_____
_____	_____	_____	_____

⌾ 12

1

Male voice 1 'You can recognise me very easily when I'm at work – I wear
   a uniform. (pause) You normally see me early in the day. I start work at
   about four o'clock in the morning and I'm finished by around eleven.
   (pause) I come to your house quite often – almost every day if a lot of
   people send you letters. (pause) Did you get it? I'm a postman.'

2

Female voice 1   'The work I'd love to do would make me quite famous. (pause) If I get my dream job you'll be able to see me every day – not in person but on TV. (pause) My dream job would be perfect for me because I'm interested in politics, current affairs and everything that's going on at the moment, so I'd love to tell everyone about it. (pause) In case you didn't guess, I'd love to be a TV news presenter.'

3

Male voice 2   'I used to have a job that gave me the chance to travel all over the world and meet thousands of people. (pause) I wasn't famous – not like a politician or movie star – but my work made me popular with people going on journeys and I always tried to be friendly and helpful and to be nice to people who were nervous. (pause) Although I travelled more than a hundred thousand miles a year, I didn't always see that much – I was too busy serving food and drinks and I often travelled by night. (pause) Did you guess? I was an airline steward.'

Give the students the chance to discuss the job after each pause and to suggest what they think it is. There is no penalty for a 'wrong' answer, the group can change their decision after stage 2 or stage 1 and the points are awarded accordingly, as explained on the recording. Ask students to say why they come to a decision, eg, 'He or she doesn't wear a uniform'.

The winning group is the one that has accumulated the most points.

6 Family relationships

Engage the students' interest in the topic by showing a photo of your own family, putting a family tree on the board, etc. (2–3 mins)

1 **People come from different family backgrounds.**
Talk with a partner and see what similarities and differences there are between your families.
These may give you some ideas:

The number of people in your household

Older or younger brothers and sisters

Aunts and uncles, nephews and nieces, cousins

Grandparents and great-grandparents

Other people

Check that the students know the vocabulary connected with immediate and extended family. Teach new items. (5–10 mins)

Instruct the students in pairs to discuss the questions they asked each other and to compare notes about similarities and differences between their families. (5–10 mins)

Engage the students' interest in the activity by telling them they are going to find out whose family is superlative! (2–3 mins)

Get the students to ask questions and give answers in open pairs across the class to find the answers to the questions. Prompt with 'How many…', 'How old…', etc, as you think appropriate. (5–10 mins)

2 **Give information and ask questions to find out which of the students in your class has:**

the largest household

the most cousins

information about great-great-grandparents

the youngest relative

the oldest living relative

Ask the students to report their findings to you; put the results on the board. (5–10 mins)

Focus on the comparative and superlative forms of adjectives, as in 'Jane has the oldest grandfather'. (5–10 mins)

Engage the students' interest by telling them they are going to listen to someone talking about how she feels about different members of her family. (2–3 mins)

Check that the students know the phrasal verbs on the list – teach alternative expressions, eg, 'look up to/admire'. (5–10 mins)

Instruct the students to discuss in pairs the phrasal verbs and the family members and speculate on which will match. (5–10 mins)

3 You are going to hear someone talking about family relationships. She uses the expressions on the left to talk about her relationships with different members of her family.
Discuss these expressions with a partner and say which you think she will use about the members of the family on the right.

'get on with'	younger brother
'look up to'	grandfather
'fall out with'	older sister
'look after'	cousin
'take after'	parents

Play the tape. Allow the students to see if they have the same answers as the speaker. (5 mins)

4 Listen to the recording.
Are your answers the same as the person talking about her family?
🔊 13

🔊 13

Young female voice 'My family? Well, like all families, we have our ups and downs. I don't think it's always possible to get on with everyone, but I do get on particularly well with my cousin Julia – we have a lot in common. I admit that I often fall out with my older sister. We're very fond of each other, but we don't always see eye-to-eye about things. My parents and I have always had a very strong relationship. They're very fair and understanding and hard-working, so I really look up to them and they respect me too. My younger brother is still only six and I often look after him. He's no trouble, most of the time. I don't think I'm like anyone else in my family except my grandfather. People tell me I have exactly the same expression as him and that I'm just as stubborn as he is, so obviously he's the one I take after.'

Play the recording again and focus on some of the words and expressions which the speaker uses to expand on the phrasal verbs in the list. These include:
'we have our ups and downs'
'we don't always see eye-to-eye'
'we have a lot in common'

Who does what in your household?

Engage the students' interest in the topic, telling them they are going to find out who does more jobs around the house. (2–3 mins)

Instruct the students individually to complete the questionnaire. (5–10 mins)

5   **Who in your household does the following things? If you are living alone at the moment, who did them when you were a child?**
Put a tick (✓) under 'I do' or write who does the things that you don't.

Household activities	I do	Who does?
Who gets up earliest?		
Who does most of the housework?		
Who watches most TV?		
Who goes to bed latest?		
Who plays the most sport?		
Who does the shopping?		
Who spends most time on the phone?		
Who eats most?		

Instruct the students in pairs to compare notes and discuss which of them does most of the things in the table (and to say who does them if the answer is not 'I do'). (5–10 mins)

6   **Compare your answers with your partners.**
Who has the most answers in the 'I do' column?
Which different people are in the 'Who does?' category?

7 Leisure time

Engage the students' interest in the topic by contrasting now (when they are studying and you are teaching) with times when you are all free. Brainstorm! Ask the students to contribute times when people normally have leisure time and put these on the board. (5 mins)

Put the appropriate preposition in front of the brainstorm items, eg, 'in the evening', 'on Sunday', 'at New Year'. (It may help to have a colour code for 'in', 'on' and 'at'.) Ask the students to suggest a pattern for the use of these prepositions and then confirm/explain that the natural pattern is:
'on a day/date'
'in a month/season'
'at a festival' (5 mins)

Note: Standard UK usage is 'at the weekend', standard USA usage is 'on the weekend', but both would be considered acceptable in the Spoken ESOL test.

Instruct the students to supply the appropriate preposition for each of the times on the list. It isn't necessary to check correct answers at this stage as the recording in activity 2 contains the answers. (2–3 mins)

Organise the students into pairs or groups and ask them to find out about each other's leisure activities. Monitor – not to correct errors during this freer activate stage, but to give any prompts which will keep the interaction flowing (eg, suggest 'other times' if students lack ideas). (5–10 mins)

1 **Work with a partner and ask and answer questions about how you spend your leisure time. Use these phrases adding 'at', 'in' or 'on' before each item:**

'at', 'in' or 'on'

	at the weekend
	in summer
	in the evening
	on Friday night
	in winter
	at New Year
	on public holidays
	at other times of the day/week/year

Engage the students' interest in listening to the tape by asking members of different pairs or groups to report briefly on the leisure activities of their partners. (5–10 mins)

Play the recording. Allow students to check that they used the appropriate preposition of time. (If you judge it necessary, play the recording a second time and address any queries which may remain over 'in', 'on' or 'at'.) (2–3 mins/5–10 mins)

2   Listen to the recording and note how the speakers use 'at', 'on' and 'in'. Do the people spend their free time in the same ways as you and your partner? 🔘 14

🔘 14

1

Male voice 'I normally work very hard during the week, so I like to take it easy at the weekend. I usually stay at home and simply relax.'

2

Female voice 'My great hobby is travel and as I have long holidays in the summer, I always go abroad.'

3

M 'I have a very full day at college, and I can't relax in the evening because I have a lot of homework assignments to do.'

4

F   'My friends and I almost always go out on Friday night; usually to a club or sometimes to a restaurant.'

5

M 'I'm mad about sports and I always go skiing and snowboarding in winter.'

6

F   'I suppose I'm quite a traditional person in many ways and I always make New Year's resolutions at New Year – I don't always keep them, though.'

7

M 'I'm the manager of a cinema, so I work on public holidays – they're the busiest times of my year.'

8

F   'I work in a factory, so I always get up very early in the morning.'

9

M 'My year is very varied, but I never miss a visit to my parents at Christmas.'

10

F   'I'm one of the rare people who enjoy Monday morning – that's because I don't work on Monday!'

I'd love to try it!

Instruct the students in their pairs or groups to discuss which of the people in the recording have leisure habits similar to theirs, then elicit responses from students at random around the class to report back on the similarities and differences. (5–10 mins)

Engage the students' interest in the topic and need for the language of expressing wishes. A good way of doing this is to take in pictures, video clips, etc, of one or two activities (ideally spectacular) which, by use of facial expression, you can indicate that you would/wouldn't like to try. Encourage students to suggest what you are thinking, eg, 'I want to go snowboarding.' (5 mins)

Focus on ways of expressing the notion of wishing to try something new. Pay attention to stress patterns and to the use of 'really' to modify what we say (eg, 'I wouldn't really like to' shows mild resistance; 'I really wouldn't like to' shows strong resistance). Instruct the students individually to complete the chart below. (5 mins)

3 **There are things we'd all love to try. Complete the questionnaire below by putting a tick (✓) in the column that expresses how you feel.**

	I'd love to try it	I wouldn't like to try it	I've already done it
Act or sing on stage			
Climb a mountain			
Learn to play a musical instrument			
Sail across an ocean			
Write a novel			
Make a parachute jump			
Travel around the world			

Organise the students into pairs or groups and ask them to compare their responses to the prompts in the questionnaire. Monitor, and encourage students to express strength of feeling through stress and intonation as well as through words and structures. (5 mins)

4 **Compare your answers with your partner – which of you is more adventurous?**

Elicit responses from the students after activity 4. Discuss who are the more/less adventurous members of the class and focus on stress and intonation patterns as effective ways of communicating this. (5–10 mins)

I'd love to try it, but…

Ask the students to suggest what it is that stops people doing things they'd really like to. Brainstorm! Put on the board some of the ideas suggested, eg, 'too scared', 'no money', etc. (2–3 mins)

Organise students into pairs/groups and ask them to suggest reasons people will give for not doing some of the things on the list. For activity 5, ask students to produce the language spoken in first-person direct speech and explain that you are going to listen to a recording to see how closely their reasons correspond to those given by the speakers. (5–10 mins)

5   You are going to hear some people talking about the things in the questionnaire in activity 3.
They would love to try them, but have never done so.
Can you guess what reasons they will give?
Talk with a partner and suggest what the people might say.

Ask students at random to produce the language they think people might use to explain why they haven't done certain things they'd like to. Make stress and intonation patterns of the speaker's sentences. (5–10 mins)

6   Listen to the people talking about why they have never done the things they would love to do.
Did you guess their reasons correctly? 📼 15

📼 15

1

Male voice 'I'd love to sing on stage but I can't – I get terrible stage fright and I'm just too nervous.'

2

Female voice 'One day I'll climb a mountain. I haven't done so yet because I've never had the time.'

3

M 'I've often thought of learning to play the piano or guitar, but to be honest I just haven't got the patience.'

4

F 'It's my dream to sail across an ocean. I haven't done it yet because I haven't got enough money – maybe one day.'

5

M 'One day I'll write a novel – not yet, because I have to finish my studies, but I will.'

6

F 'My ambition is to make a parachute jump. I'd love it! The problem is, my family won't let me.'

7

M 'I'd really like to travel all around the world. You'll never guess why I haven't done – it's because I've got three cats and I can't bear to leave them.'

Play the recording and get the students to check if their reasons were similar to those given by the speakers. Play the tape again to focus on individual utterances and to give students the chance to hear and repeat the stress and intonation patterns used. (5–10 mins)

8 I've done it!

Engage the students' interest in the topic. You may have a diploma or sports medal that you can show the class, or you could use photos of people who have just won a game or achieved some other personal triumph.

Ask the students to look at the questionnaire in activity 1 and individually to tick the appropriate column. Emphasise that the categories are to be interpreted broadly and 'practical skill', 'difficult journey', etc, are open to the students' own interpretation. (5 mins)

1 **We have all done things we are pleased with.**
   Which of these have you done?
   Put a tick (✓) in the column that applies to you.

Achievements	'I've done it'	'I don't think I'll ever do it'	'I'm hoping to do it soon'
Passed an important exam			
Made something useful			
Won a sports prize			
Earned or saved money to buy something			
Learnt a practical skill			
Completed a difficult journey			
Learnt to play a musical instrument			
Other things			

Ask the students to work in pairs to ask and answer questions about their past or potential achievements. It is probable that the students will make mistakes when attempting to use several verb tenses in the same interaction but it is best not to correct them now. Take note of any errors which impede communication and which may usefully be the focus of a study phase at some point in the near future. (5–10 mins)

2 **Now work with a partner. Compare the things in activity 1 each of you has done or hope to do. Give details of when you did it or hope to do it.**

Focus on the words we use to describe achievements. Ask the students to look at the list of verbs and individually or in pairs to provide the nouns and adjectives (if there are any) which come from the same root. Stress that it is not important if there are some words they don't know; they'll hear the answers in the recording. (2–3 mins)

3   Here are words we often use to talk about things we've done and are pleased with. You are going to hear people talking about the things they've done from the list above.
Can you fill in the missing words below?

Verb	Noun	Adjective
to achieve	achievement	achievable (not in tapescript)
to enjoy	enjoyment	enjoyable
to succeed	success	successful
to persist	persistence	persistent

Play the recording to allow the students to check their answers.

You can usefully expand this activity by asking the students which of these adjectives – and any similar ones they can think of – apply to themselves. This can be conducted as a group activity with all the students being invited to contribute. You may also like to note a few adjectives you think apply to you and invite the students to guess what you have written. (5–10 mins)

4   Listen to the recording to check your answers. 🔊 16

🔊 16
1

Female voice 'Passing my driving test after failing three times was my greatest achievement.'
2

Male voice 'For me, there's nothing so enjoyable as seeing my garden look its best – that's true enjoyment.'
3

F   'People tell me I'm a successful teacher and perhaps they're right – my greatest success so far was helping all my students pass their exams last year.'
4

M   'I'm a sports coach and people often ask me for advice. It's simple: be persistent and you'll win. Persistence always pays.'

Introduce the topic of ambition. It will be helpful to clarify the different connotations of the key words 'hope', 'plan' and 'expect'. 'Plan' suggests a very active and specific set of future intentions; 'expect' has a high degree of probability; 'hope' sounds possible rather than probable. You may like to offer one or two of your own hopes, plans and expectations as examples. (5 mins)

Ask the students individually to make a few brief notes about their own future hopes, plans and expectations. (5 mins)

5   **And what about your future ambitions?**
    What do you hope, plan and expect to do in these areas of your life?

	Hope	Plan	Expect
Occupation			
Academic studies			
Family			
Leisure			
Languages			

Ask the students to work in pairs to compare their answers about their ambitions. (5–10 mins)

6   **Compare your ambitions with your partner.**

Now ask the students to listen to the recording of people speaking about their future hopes, plans and expectations. Play the recording and ask the students to make notes about things the speakers say which are the same as or different from what they and their partner said. (5 mins)

7   **Listen to these people talking about their future ambitions.**
    Make a note of their hopes, plans and expectations. 🔘 17

	Hope	Plan	Expect
1			
2			
3			
4			
5			

🔘 17

1

Male voice 'I'm a journalist. I hope to be the editor of a national newspaper one day and I plan to leave my present paper as soon as I can. What do I actually expect? It's a difficult question – I'll probably stay in the same job for the rest of my career, I'm afraid.'

2

Female voice 1 'I hope to pass my exams and then I plan to go to university. I usually get fairly good grades so I expect to pass.'

3

M 'I plan to get married next year and I hope I'll have three or four children. I expect I'll find that it's pretty difficult to be a parent.'

4

F 'I love windsurfing and I plan to enter the national championships next year. To be frank, I expect to finish low in the competition, but, of course, I hope to win!'

5

M 'I plan to learn several different languages and I hope to be fluent in some of them. I expect that what will happen is that I'll start, but I'll never really learn them properly.'

In a group activity, ask the students to tell you which hopes, plans and expectations they, their partners and the speakers all spoke about. Ask how likely they think these ambitions are to be realised and how this might happen. (5–10 mins)

Test practice

The organisation of the test practice is a matter for your judgement in the particular teaching situation you are in. With larger classes, it can be difficult to use the practice test as an activity in class time. You can ask the students to practise in pairs, with one adopting the role of interlocutor, but if it is possible to conduct the practice exercise (and at some stage a full practice test) yourself or have a fellow teacher do so, it will be valuable test preparation.

(This type of task would normally take only a few minutes in the test itself and one of the test skills to cultivate is a fluent exchange of information/comment in a short time.)

Test practice – Achiever

**The following questions are similar to those you will be asked in Part 1
of the Spoken ESOL test at the Achiever level.**
The interlocutor will start by saying:
'… and now I'd like to ask you some questions about yourself.'

Daily Life
'Tell me something about breakfast time in your house or flat.'

'What do you usually do on weekday mornings?'

'How do you spend your evenings during the week?'

'Which places do you often go to at the weekend?'

Music
'Tell me about the kind of music you like.'

'What were your music classes at school like?'

'Do you prefer live or recorded music? Why?'

'Which musical instrument would you like to play? Why?'

Keeping Fit
'Is keeping fit important to you? Why?'

'How do you try to keep fit?'

'What kind of food do you like to eat?'

'Which sports do you like playing? Why do you like them?'

English Learning
'When and where did you start learning English?'

'What's the most difficult part of learning English?'

'What do you like best about learning English?'

'Tell me about your English class.'

Friends
'Tell me something about the friends you have here.'

'How do you keep in contact with old friends?'

'Do you think you are a good friend? Why/why not?'

'Do you prefer to go on holiday with friends or your family? Why?'

Test practice – Communicator

The following questions are similar to those you will be asked in Part 1 of the Spoken ESOL test at the Communicator level.
The interlocutor will start by saying:
'… to start I'd like to ask you a few questions about yourself.'

Neighbourhood
'How long have you lived in your neighbourhood?'

'Could you tell me what you like most about the area where you live?'

'Is there anything you would like to change about the place where you live?'

'Can you tell me about the people who live in your neighbourhood?'

Education
'What have you enjoyed most about your education so far?'

'Which subjects at school did you find most interesting? Why?'

'What are your earliest memories of school?'

'Are there any teachers you especially remember?'

Hobbies and interests
'What hobbies and interests did you have as a young child?'

'How do you mostly spend your leisure time these days?'

'Would you describe yourself as an active person? Why/why not?'

'Tell me about the kinds of things that you enjoy reading.'

Work
'What job do you do/do you hope to do?'

'What ambitions do you have for your future career?'

'Would you prefer to work for yourself or for a company? Why?'

'What would be the ideal job for you, do you think?'

Relationships
'Can you tell me something about the most important people in your life?'

'How good are you at keeping in touch with old friends?'

'Do you think it's easier or more difficult to make friends as you get older?'

'What qualities in a friend are important to you?'

Part 2 Social situations

In Part 2 of this book the focus is on social situations, and the language skills needed to communicate in a natural and polite way. In the Spoken ESOL test, the candidate acts out social situations with the interlocutor. The interlocutor may adopt a different persona, but the candidate will always be himself or herself. The interlocutor will explain the context, the situation and will say whether the candidate should respond or start.

At the Achiever and Communicator levels, the examiner will not expect the candidate to speak without mistakes, although an ability to recognise and correct errors will be credited by the examiner. Students should be advised that if they make a mistake, they should continue talking. Candidates should be able to communicate formally or informally as the situation requires. They should use language appropriate to the location and the person with whom they are speaking. Stress and intonation patterns make a significant contribution to successful communication in Part 2 situations – remind your students that in acting out real-life situations, it isn't just what you say, but the way that you say it.

The units in Part 2 include a wide range of practice tasks that cover situations a candidate is likely to encounter in everyday life and also in the test. These include polite forms of greeting and saying goodbye, asking for and giving directions, shopping, ordering in a restaurant, apologising and forgiving in a range of situations, and accepting and refusing offers. The recordings which support the units give actual models of language functions which your students can incorporate into their own repertoire of language.

Unlike Part 1 of the test, Part 2 requires the candidate to initiate as well as respond. It will be useful to give students as much practice as possible in this, and the pair/group activities are designed for this purpose. It is probable that you will find yourself correcting mistakes less during the pair/group activities in Part 2. The most important skill for students to develop is that of maintaining interaction, at times in spite of mistakes (which are, after all, a feature of native-speaker production). Close monitoring will enable you to note any persistent errors and make these a focus of a future lesson.

2

2

Part 2 Social situations

It will help you to communicate confidently if you know the natural and polite way to speak to people in social situations. You may want to use English in many different social situations: in shops, in cafés and restaurants, when you travel by train, bus or plane, at the cinema or theatre, in hotels, at a friend's home and so on. The units that follow will help you build the language skills you need for this.

In Part 2 of the Spoken ESOL test the interlocutor will give you different social situations – some where you must start the conversation and some where you must respond. The interlocutor sometimes plays the role of someone else, saying, for example, 'I am a friend', or 'I am a shopkeeper'. You, however, do not play a role – you are always you.

Tips from the examiners

In order to express yourself effectively you need to think about a number of things:

What language functions are you being asked to use?

Listen carefully and make sure you understand the situation and what you are being asked to do. Do you need to apologise for something? Are you meant to request something? Be sure you understand what is required. Then decide what you want to say.

Where are you?

Is the situation taking place in a shop, in your home or somewhere else? How would you speak in these places in real life?

Who are you talking to?

Make sure you know what role the interlocutor is playing. Are you talking to a friend or a stranger? Someone older or younger than you? These things will affect what you say and how you say it.

What are your views and feelings?

At the Achiever and Communicator levels, you may be given situations where you need to express your opinions or feelings. The interlocutor may tell you that you are happy or that you feel ill. What you think and how you feel will affect what you say.

1 Suggesting, proposing and advising

Engage the students' interest by taking items out of a bag and making suggestions using 'Would you like to…?' (Possible items: tennis racquet – 'play tennis', goggles – 'go swimming', cup – 'have a cup of coffee', etc)

Elicit the structure 'Would you like to…?' Write it on the board. (2 mins)

Tell the students they have a week's holiday next week. Ask them to look at the pictures. Get them to practise suggesting these ideas to a partner – they can expand if they like: ('Would you like to go to the cinema?' 'Which film would you like to see?')   (2–5 mins)

1   **You and some friends have a week's holiday.
    Would you like to do any of these things?**

    Suggest the ideas in the pictures to your friends using this phrase:

    'Would you like + infinitive.'

    For example:

    'Would you like to go to the cinema tonight?'

    'Would you like to see a film this week?'

    Play the recording and find out if any suggestions are different.
    Check for the error 'Would you like going?' (2–5 mins)

2   **Listen to the questions and suggestions on the recording.
    Are yours different?** 🔊 18

🔊 18
    1

**Female voice 'Would you like to have a meal in that Chinese restaurant
    tonight?'**
Male voice 'Mmm. I'd love to.'
    2
M 'Would you like to go to the beach on Monday?'
F 'Oh yes! That'd be great.'
    3
M 'Would you like to come to Angie's party with me on Saturday?'
F 'I'm sorry, I can't. I'm going away this weekend.'
    4
M 'Would you like to take a trip to the mountains on Sunday?'
F 'Yes, I would. That's a brilliant idea.'

Brainstorm words for sports and other activities offered at a sports club.
Write them all up on the right side of the board. (2 mins)

Suggest doing a couple of these activities to one or two students using:
'How/what about + gerund or noun?'
'How do you feel about + gerund or noun?' (2 mins)

3 **Suggest that you and your partner take part in the different activities at the sports centre opposite. Use these phrases:**

'How/what about + gerund or noun?'

'How do you feel about + gerund or noun?'

For example:

'How/what about playing tennis this afternoon?'

'How do you feel about a game of tennis this afternoon?'

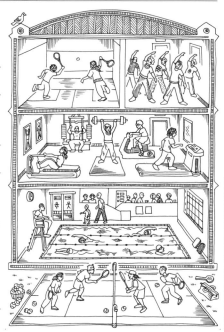

Elicit these structures from the students and write them up on the left side of the board.

Get the students to suggest doing the activities on the board using these structures. Tell them to include a time ('tonight', 'at six o'clock', 'next Saturday'), and to reply to the suggestions. (2–5 mins)

After they've practised, ask them to listen to the recording and check if the answers were similar to their own. (2–5 mins)

4 **Listen to some of the suggestions and replies on the recording. Are they similar to yours?** 📟 19

📟 19

1

Female voice 1 'How about going swimming today?'
Female voice 2 'That would be nice. What time?'
F1 'Two o'clock?'
F2 'Yes, that's fine.'

2

Male voice 1 'How do you feel about a game of squash tonight?'
Male voice 2 'Not tonight, thanks. I'm too tired.'

3

Female voice 'What about going to the gym tomorrow?'
Male voice 'Good idea. I need some exercise.'

Ask a couple of students if they are free – tonight, on Sunday or next week.

If they say 'yes', make some suggestions using the following structures:
'Why don't we + infinitive (without "to")?'
'Let's + infinitive (without "to").

Elicit these structures and draw their attention to the omission of 'to'. (2 mins)

Tell the students to move around the class with their diaries and a pen asking each other what they are doing on certain days and suggesting ideas. Get them to expand (time, place, etc) their dialogues. They should try to interact with all the other students. You should also be part of this group and join in. **(15 mins)**

5   **Make suggestions to your friends about what to do next week.**
Put the arrangements in your diary below.
Suggest your ideas using these phrases:

'Why don't we + infinitive (without "to")?'

'Let's + infinitive (without "to").'

For example:

'Why don't we go for a walk on Wednesday afternoon?'

'Let's try that new pizza café on Saturday night.'

Diary	am	pm
Monday		
Tuesday		
Wednesday		
Thursday		
Friday		
Saturday		
Sunday		

Tell the students you are going to play a recording of some friends planning their diaries for next week. Ask them to try and remember as many of the replies as they can. They can write them down if they like. **(5–10 mins)**

6   **Listen to the recording.**
Some friends are planning their diaries for next week.
Try to remember as many of the replies as you can.
Compare the replies you remember with those your partner remembers.
🔲 20

🔲 20

1

Male voice   **'Why don't we go to the Timepiece Club on Wednesday? You'd love it.'**

Female voice   'Okay, then. Why not?'

2

F   **'Let's stay in and watch TV tonight.'**

M   'Oh no. I'd much rather go out.'

3

F **'Why don't you come round for a meal on Thursday?'**

M 'I'd love to. But I can't come before eight-thirty, I'm afraid.'

F **'Don't worry. We usually eat late anyway.'**

4

Female voice 1 'It's such lovely weather at the moment. Let's take a walk along the river on Tuesday afternoon.'

Female voice 2 'Alright then. I'll meet you outside college at two.'

5

M 'Ann's really fed up at the moment. Why don't we take her to that concert on Friday evening?'

F 'That's an excellent idea. She'd love it.'

Advising

Pretend you've got a terrible toothache. Ask the students for advice. (5 mins)

Divide the board into two. Ask the students to brainstorm all the people who give them advice (eg, doctor, parents, friends, teacher, neighbour). Write them up on one side. Then ask who the students give advice to (eg, brother, sister, best friend). Write these up on the other side of the board.

Ask the students to think of somebody they have recently given advice to. Get them to tell their partners. (2 mins)

7 Think of somebody you have given advice to. Who was it? What advice did you give? Tell your partner.

Tell the students to look at the people in the pictures. Ask them what advice they would give them, using the structure 'Why don't you + infinitive (without "to")?' Elicit answers after a couple of minutes. (5 mins)

8 Now look at these people. What advice would you give them? Use this phrase:

'Why don't you + infinitive (without "to")?'

Now play the recording and allow the students to check their answers.

9 Listen to the recording. Is your advice the same? 🔊 21

🔊 21

1

Female voice 'Why don't you open the window?'

2

Male voice 'Why don't you lie down for a while?'

3

F 'Why don't you get a haircut?'

4

M 'Why don't you put your sunglasses on?'

Tell the students to look at the problems of the people in the next set of pictures.

Ask the students to think of good advice using the structures 'You should…', 'You'd better…' (urgent situations only) and 'You ought to…'. The students can exchange ideas with a partner before feeding back as a whole class. Correct any errors. (5–10 mins)

**10 Now look at these people. What advice would you give them?
Use the phrases:**

'You should + infinitive (without "to").'

'You'd better + infinitive (without "to").' (in urgent situations only)

'You ought to + infinitive.'

For example:

'I think you should go to the dentist.'

'You'd better see the dentist.'

'You ought to take an aspirin.'

Ask the students to think of two problems they have at the moment. Get them to ask their partners for advice. Then have a feedback session for the best and worst pieces of advice received. (5–10 mins)

**11 Think of or invent two problems you have at the moment.
Tell your partner about them and ask for some advice.**

What would you do if you were me?

Explain the word 'shopaholic' (a compulsive shopper). Tell the students they are going to listen to a shopaholic talking about her problem. Ask them to think of suitable advice for her. (5–10 mins)

Play the recording.

12 Listen to a woman talking. She's a 'shopaholic'. 🔊 22

🔊 22

Female voice 'I've always loved shopping and to be honest I think I'm turning into a bit of a shopaholic. Any spare time I've got, I don't go swimming or to the cinema. I head straight for the shops. Even on holiday I can't help myself. Everyone else is enjoying the beach, lying under a sunshade, relaxing, and I find myself getting irritable and that urge comes over me. I must go shopping!'

'When it was just window-shopping it wasn't so bad. I was happy just looking at everything, strolling around the department stores, comparing prices and everything. People thought I was wasting my time, but at least it was harmless.

'Now though, I think it's more than a harmless bit of fun. I actually can't go into a shop without buying something. Clothes are my worst thing. If I see something I like, I've just got to have it. It's ridiculous really.

'I find myself buying stuff in the supermarket which I don't need. I can't resist the temptation of a bargain or an offer. But what can I do…?'

Elicit advice for the woman from the students. Discuss their ideas.

13 **Now think of some advice to help solve her problem.
Use this phrase:**

'If I were you, I would/I'd + infinitive (without "to").'

For example:

'If I were you, I'd leave my wallet at home.'

'If I were you, I'd stay in bed!'

14 **Compare your advice with your partner's.**

Use the following additional practice activity for suggesting and advising:
Each student has three cards with a problem situation on each. The students walk around the room giving and receiving advice for their problems. At the end, the students tell their partners about the best piece of advice they've received. (5–10 mins)

2 Asking for information and directions

Draw three columns on the board. Write these column headings: 'shoe shop', 'railway station', 'classroom'. Brainstorm the kinds of information you might ask for in each place. Write it up on the board. (5–10 mins)

Put the class into small groups. Tell them they're going to listen to people talking. Ask them to think about where the people are and if they are talking to a stranger or not. Pause the tape after each conversation and let them discuss their ideas in groups.

Then get feedback before confirming and playing the tape a second time. (5–10 mins)

1   Listen to the recording. Where do you think these people are? Are they talking to someone they know or to a stranger? 🔲 23

🔲 23

1

Male voice 'Sorry to bother you, but do you know what time the museum opens?'
Female voice 'Yes, look. It says on the board. Nine-fifteen.'
M 'Oh, I didn't notice it, thanks.'
F   'Not at all.'

2

Female voice 1 'I'm looking for a not-too-expensive hotel which is close to the city centre. Can you help me, please?'
Female voice 2 'Yes, of course. Here's a list of hotels recommended by the tourist board.'
F1 'Oh, that's great. Thank you.'
F2 'You're welcome.'

3

M 'I was wondering if you've got this in a medium size in blue?'
F   'Just a moment, sir. I'll go and check.'
M 'Thank you.'

4

F 'Have you got any idea where I can get a picture dictionary in Japanese?'
M   'Hm, let me see. Why not try that new bookshop on the corner?'
F 'Good idea. I will. Thanks.'

2   Discuss your ideas in a small group.

Get the students to look at the opening phrases for asking for information and to decide which you'd use with a friend and which with a stranger. (5 mins)

3   Here are some useful opening phrases when asking for information. Which ones would you use with a friend and which with a stranger?

'Excuse me. I wonder if you can/could help me?' stranger

'Hey, do you know where/what/why/how … ?' friend

'I'm sorry to bother you, but could you … ?' stranger

'I know this sounds stupid, but … ?' friend

'You don't know where/when/if/what …, do you?' friend

'There's something I want to know … ' friend

'Have you got any idea if/why/how/what … ?' stranger

'I hope you don't mind me/my asking, but do you know … ?' stranger

Check their answers and explain why it's important to choose a phrase which is appropriate to the situation.

Tell the students to look at the pictures and think about what the people might want to know. Then ask them to practise with their partners using the study phrases. Move around the class monitoring. (5 mins)

4   **Look at the pictures. What might these people want to know? Practise asking for some information with a partner.**

Then play the tape and find out how similar their requests are.

5   **Listen to the dialogues on the recording. How similar are they to yours?** 🔊 24

🔊 24

1

Female voice 'Can you tell me what time the last showing of *Present Danger* is, please?'

Male voice 'Eight forty-five.'

F   **'Thank you.'**

2

F   **'I'm sorry to bother you, but do you know if this bus stops at Blackpool, please?'**

M   'Yes, it does.'

F   **'Thanks.'**

3

F   **'Have you got any idea what "Toad in the Hole" is?'**

M   'I haven't got a clue, I'm afraid.'

F   **'Oh dear!'**

4

M   **'Excuse me, I wonder if you can help me.'**

F   'Well, I'll try.'

M   **'Well, I'm looking for a biography of Alfred Jarry.'**

F   'Our biography section is upstairs. In alphabetical order.'

M   **'Thanks a lot.'**

F   'Not at all.'

Giving information

Tell the students to listen to the recording and to decide how the people answer. They can compare their answers with a partner before you play the recording again and elicit the right answers from the whole class.
(5 mins)

**6 Listen to some people giving information on the recording.
Do they answer positively, do they use delaying tactics to gain
time to think or do they avoid answering altogether?** 📼 25

📼 25
1
**Female voice 'I know this sounds stupid, but do you know what
"handkerchief" is in French?'**
Male voice 'Hm, let me see. It's "mouchoir", isn't it?'
2
M 'Could you tell me where the locker room is?'
F   'Yes, of course. It's at the end of the corridor.'
3
F 'You don't know where Anna keeps her records, do you?'
M   'No idea. Sorry.'
4
F 'I'm looking for a poster for my 12-year-old nephew. Have you got any ideas?'
M   'No problem. There' s a whole rack of football posters over there. Is he into football?'
F 'Yes, he loves it. That's a great idea. Thanks.'

7 Compare your ideas with your partner.

Look at the delaying and negative techniques with the whole class.
Ask the class when they think they might need to use them. (5–10 mins)

**8 Here are some positive and negative responses and delaying
techniques to use when giving information.
In which situations do you think you might need to use them?**

'I wonder if you know/could tell me where/ have any idea if … ?'

Positive

'Yes, of course.'

'No problem.'

'That's easy. You just … '

'You've asked the right person!'

Negative

'Sorry, I've no idea.'

'Haven't got a clue, I'm afraid.'

'I'm not really/totally/altogether sure about that.'

'I'd like/love to help you, but I honestly don't know.'

'Sorry. I can't help you, I'm afraid.'

Delaying

'Now, let me see … '

'Hm. Just let me think for a moment …'

'That's an interesting question … '

'Hang on a second while I have a think.'

Tell the students to listen to the recording and to say what answers they might get. (5 mins)

9 **Listen to the recording of people asking for information. What answers do you think they will get?** 🔲 26

🔲 26

1

Male voice 'Hey, how do I use these chopsticks?'

2

Female voice 'You don't know who wrote *David Copperfield*, do you?'

3

M **'Have you got any idea what the capital of Borneo is?'**

4

F 'There's something I want to know. How old do you have to be to drive in your country?'

5

M **'Excuse me, but do you know whose face it is on the American dollar?'**

6

F 'Do you happen to know when the Great Wall of China was built?'

7

M **'Have you any idea which language they speak in Iran?'**

Asking for and giving directions

Find a clear map of any town or city centre. Copy it. Get the students to start at a given point. Ask them to direct you to points on the map using these phrases:
'Excuse me, could you tell me where the college is, please?'
… tell me the way to the college, please?'
… direct me to the college, please?'
'I'm sorry to bother you, but do you know where the college is, please?
Then, in pairs, get them to ask for and give directions using the map. (5 mins)

10 **Look at the map of the city centre, which your teacher will give you. Find the starting point, which is marked with an 'x'. Your teacher will ask for directions. Using the map, try to help.**

Ask the students to match the directions and the pictures. This can be done individually or in pairs. Help with vocabulary. (5 mins)

11 Now work with your partner. Ask for and give directions to different places on the map. Ask your teacher to help with new vocabulary.

'It's on the left.'

'Go straight on/ahead./Keep on going./Carry on.'

'Take the second turning on your right/left.'

'Go around the roundabout and take the third exit.'

'Take the left fork at the junction.'

'Go past the tennis courts.'

'Go to the end of this/the road.'

'Go over/across the crossroads.'

'Go to the top of the hill.'

'Cross over the bridge.'

'It's on the corner.'

We often finish giving directions by saying:

'You can't miss it!'
'You're bound to see it!'
Look at the new vocabulary in activity 11. Ask the class which of the features mentioned – roundabouts, tennis courts, crossroads, etc – can be found in your town. Explain any they don't know. (10–15 mins)
Get the students to ask for and give directions (tell each other how they get from home to class, from the station to the bank, etc). They should use as many of the expressions they have learnt as possible.

12 How many of these places can you find in your town or city? Ask for and give directions to places in your town:

from your classroom to the bus stop

from the station to the bank

from the post office to the park

from your home to the nearest chemist

from your home to the cinema

3 Complaining, apologising and forgiving
Complaining

Write the words 'annoyed', 'upset', 'angry' and 'furious' randomly on the board. Ask the class to rank them in terms of strength of feeling. (2 mins)

Tell the students they're going to listen to four people on the recording. Which word best describes how they are feeling?

1 **Listen to the people on the recording. How angry do you think they are? How important is the tone of voice in helping you decide?** 📼 27

📼 27

1

Female voice (angry) 'Oh, honestly, I wish you'd told me before.'

2

Male voice (annoyed) 'I've been waiting over half an hour.'

3

F (furious) 'This is the worst hotel I've ever stayed at!'

4

M (upset) 'I don't like complaining, but you promised it would be ready today.'

Tell the class that when we want to complain in English, we try to adopt a polite tone of voice and to use a 'softly, softly' approach wherever possible. Introduce these expressions, which help this approach:
'I hate/don't like complaining/to complain, but…'
'I'm sorry to have to say this, but…'
'I'm afraid there's a bit of a problem…'
'Look, I'm sorry, but I must complain about…' (5 mins)

Tell the students to look at the pictures of customers in a restaurant and to roleplay in pairs. One student is the waiter, the other the customer. The customer uses the 'softly, softly' phrases to complain to the waiter. Move around the class monitoring. Make sure the customers and waiters swap roles. (5–10 mins)

2 **With your partner, pretend to be the people in the pictures. They are all complaining to a waiter. Take it in turns to be customer and waiter.**

Play the recording of people complaining about the situations in the pictures.

3 **Listen to the recording. Were your conversations similar to the dialogues?** 📼 28

📟 28

1

Female voice **'I'm afraid there's a bit of a problem. I've found this beetle in my soup.'**

2

Male voice 'Sorry to complain, but this glass is cracked.'

3

M 'I hate complaining, but this meat's so tough, it's inedible.'

4

F 'Look, I'm sorry, but I must complain about this coffee. It's awful.'

Get the students to match the problem situations in activity 4 and the places where they might find them. (5 mins)

---

4   **Match the complaint and the place you might hear it.**

1 hotel	4 'The sound's terrible!'
2 railway station	1 'It's a horrible view from the window!'
3 taxi	2 'I definitely reserved a seat.'
4 cinema	5 'Not more overtime!'
5 at work	3 'Fifty pounds? You must be joking!'

Divide the class in two. They are going to play 'Shopkeepers'. (15–20 mins)

Half the class are shopkeepers. The shopkeepers should sit down in separate places and wait for their customers to come into their shop. They should be polite and as helpful as possible, offering a solution to the problem.

---

5   **You are going to play 'Shopkeepers'. Split up into two groups.
Group A: You are shopkeepers. Sit down and wait for customers to come into your 'shop'. Try to be as polite and helpful as possible. Find a solution to your customers' problems.
Group B: You are customers. Go from shop to shop and complain about the following things:**

shirt (£25.00)	small hole on the back of the collar
shoes (£18.99)	heel came off
milk (35p)	tastes sour, past its sell-by date
alarm clock (£8.59)	not loud enough to wake you up
sweater (£35.00)	shrank in the wash
CD headphones (£20.00)	buzzing in one ear
peaches (40p)	rotten in the middle

Now the students swap roles.

6   **Group A and Group B swap roles. Group B: Go from shop to shop and complain about the following things:**

bottle of cola (£1.00)	strange taste
dry-cleaned coat (£3.50)	stain is still there
video (£12.99)	'snow' effect in the middle
towel (£15.00)	dye came out when washed
book (£8.99)	two middle pages are blank
frozen pizza (£3.85)	found a hair in it

When the activity has finished ask the whole class the following questions:
'Who was the most helpful shopkeeper?' 'Who was the angriest customer?' 'Which shop would you never go back to again?'

Apologising

Walk around the class and do things for which you must apologise (knock a book onto the floor, bump into a desk, drop something near a student, etc). After each incident use one of the following expressions:
'Sorry.'
'I'm so sorry.'
'I'm really sorry.'
'I'm ever so sorry.'
'Terribly sorry.' (2–5 mins)

Elicit these phrases from the class and write them on the board.

Tell the class that these ways of apologising can be used in both informal and formal situations.

Get the students to read the sentences and to match the situation and the apology. (5 mins)

7   **Read the sentences. Match the statements and the apologies.**

1 'Hey, that's my bag!'	2 'I'm so sorry. I've called the wrong number.'
2 'There's nobody here with that name.'	3 'I'm really sorry. I missed the bus.'
3 'You're late again.'	1 'Terribly sorry. I thought it was mine.'
4 'Ouch!'	5 'I'm ever so sorry. I'll get you another one.'
5 'You've lost it?'	4 'Sorry. I didn't see you there.'

Check and correct their answers. Explain that other ways of apologising are for more formal or serious situations.

8 **Look at these expressions used in more formal or serious situations:**

'I can't tell you how sorry I am.'

'I really must apologise.'

'I just don't know what to say.'

'I'm dreadfully sorry. What more can I say?'

Play the recording and ask the students to say why the people are apologising and what they think has happened. How serious are the situations? (5 mins)

9 **Listen to the recording. Why are these people apologising? What do you think has happened? How serious are the situations?** 🔊 29

🔊 29

1

Male voice 'So sorry to keep you waiting, Mrs Edwards. We had an emergency this morning.'
Female voice 'Oh, that's alright. I'm just glad you can see me now because it's started playing up again.'

2

F 'You promised me that you'd fixed it, but it went and broke down when I was miles from anywhere. I didn't have my mobile with me either. I was lucky someone was passing.'
M 'I'm really very sorry about this. We'll go and sort it out straight away.'
F 'I should hope so too.'

3

Female voice 1 'I hate complaining, but just look at it. It's green!'
Female voice 2 'Oh, not green exactly. More a greeny-brown. I think it suits you actually.'
F1 'Well, I don't.'
F2 'I'm sorry about that. Do you want me to colour it again with a deeper brown?'
F1 'Yes, please.'

Get the students to roleplay the situations in the pictures. They should swap roles after each one. (5–10 mins)

10 Look at the two people in each picture opposite. With your partner, each take a role and act out the situations.

Forgiving

Play the recording and ask the students to listen to the replies the people make.

Ask the whole class to supply the answers. Play again if necessary. (5 mins)

11 Listen to the recording. How do the people reply to the apologies? 🔊 30

🔊 30

1

Male voice 'I'm sorry, I've eaten all the grapes.'

Female voice 'That's alright. I'm glad you enjoyed them.'

2

F 'I must apologise for being so unhelpful.'

M 'Don't worry about it. It's not your fault.'

3

F 'I'm so sorry to have forgotten it.'

M 'Honestly, it doesn't matter.'

4

M 'How could I have been so stupid?'

F 'Please think no more of it.'

Look at the expressions for forgiving in activity 12 as a whole class.

12 Look at some different ways of forgiving:

'That's/It's alright.'

'It (really) doesn't matter.'

'Don't worry about it.'

'Forget it.'

'No problem.'

'Think no more of it.'

'I don't want to hear any more about it.'

This final activity should activate all the language studied in Unit 3.
Get the students to swap partners and walk around monitoring,
advising and correcting. (5–10 mins)

**13 You and your partner are neighbours. Look at the problems in the
picture. With your partner, act out the situations and try to find solutions
to them. Remember you must complain, apologise and perhaps forgive!
Take turns to play the roles.**

Have a general brief feedback session. Ask them how many solutions
they found to the problems. (2–5 mins)

4 Offering, accepting and refusing

Offering

Engage the students' interest by opening a bag in which you have various items (sweets, an orange, a can of soft drink, etc). Walk around the class offering the students different items using 'Would you like...?' and 'Do you want...?'

Ask the students to tell you how you began your offers. Write the two phrases on the board. (2–4 mins)

Ask the students in pairs to offer each other the things in the pictures in activity 1. (2–4 mins)

1   **Look at these pictures. Work with a partner and offer each other the things in the pictures.**

Ask the students to look at the pictures in activity 2. They all show examples of offering. Ask them what's being offered – a thing, an action or both? (5 mins)

2   **Look at the pictures opposite. Talk with a partner and say what you think people are offering each other – is it a thing, an action or both? Put a tick (✓) below to say which it is in each picture.**

Picture	Thing	Action	Both
A	✓		
B		✓	
C			✓
D			✓
E	✓		
F		✓	

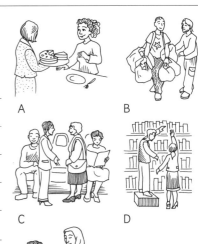

Now ask the students to listen to the recording and match the conversations and the pictures. Get them to compare their answers with a partner.

You can then play the recording again and check with the whole class.

3 Listen to the recording. Check your answers. 🔊 31

🔊 31

1

Female voice 1 'Mmm, that looks lovely.'
Female voice 2 'Would you like a slice?'
F1 'Yes, please. I'd love one.'
F2 'There you are.'

2

Male voice 1 'Your bags look heavy.
Male voice 2 'Yes, actually they are.'
M 'Can I help you with them?'
M 'Oh, well. That's very kind of you, thanks.'

3

F1 'Why don't you have my seat?'
F2 'That's very nice of you, dear. Thanks.'

4

M 'Can you reach?'
F 'I don't think I can, actually.'
M 'Let me get it for you.'
F 'Well, thanks. It's the thick one in the middle.'

5

F 'That's £29 then, please.'
M 'Can I pay by credit card?'
F 'Of course. Sign here, please. Do you want to use my pen?'
M 'Yes, thanks.'

6

M1 'Where are you going?'
M2 'I've got to get to the station.'
M1 'Why don't I give you a lift?'
M2 'Now that's an offer I won't refuse!'

Tell the students they are going to look at different ways of offering to do something for someone, eg, posting a letter for a friend.
'Let me post it for you.'
'Shall I post it for you?'
'Why don't I post it for you?'
'If you like, I can post it for you.'
'Would you like me to post it for you?'
'How about me/my posting it for you?' (5–8 mins)

Tell the students to work in pairs. Ask them to use the prompts and improvise dialogues for these situations. Ask them to use the language they've just studied. First check that all the vocabulary is clear. (5–10 mins)

4 **Work with your partner. Use the prompts and roleplay the situations.**
Student A: You are going abroad for the first time next week.
Student B: You are a friend who offers to help.

choose clothes and pack

lift to airport

confirm flight

look after flat

feed pet fish

Student A: You are giving a housewarming party.
Student B: You are a neighbour who offers to help.

write/send invitations

clean /decorate house

shop

prepare food

borrow CDs, cassettes

Accepting and refusing

Ask the students to listen to the recording and decide what the
people are offering to do. Also ask them to remember as many
of the expressions as possible. Get them to compare their answers
with their partners. (5–10 mins)

5 **Listen to the recording. What are the speakers offering to do?**
Discuss your ideas with a partner and then listen again to check
your answers. 🔲 32

🔲 32
  1
Male voice 'If you like, I'll pick you up around seven.'
Female voice 'That would be great, thanks.'
  2
Female voice 1 'Shall I do the other rooms as well as the bathroom
  and kitchen?'
Female voice 2 'Well, if you don't mind – thanks.'
  3
M 'How about me knocking something together for us tonight?'
F 'You?!'
M 'Well, I do a very nice spaghetti, you know.'
F 'Well … Okay then.'
  4
F1 'Would you like me to do your back for you?'
F2 'I must admit it does feel very sore and stiff.'
F1 'Come on, then.'
F2 'Well, thank you, that would be nice.'

Now ask the students to listen to recording 33 and decide whether the people accept or refuse the offer. Ask them how many expressions they can remember and play the recording again if they need help.

6 Listen to the recording. Can you tell if the speakers are accepting or refusing offers? Try to remember the expressions they use. 📟 33

📟 33

1

Male voice 'Do you want me to drive you there?'
Female voice 'It's okay, thanks. I'll walk.'

2

Female voice 1 'Why not borrow my black dress for the party?'
Female voice 2 'Are you sure? Well, thanks.'

3

Male voice 1 'You look terrible. Can I get you anything?'
Male voice 2 'I'm alright, thanks.'

4

M 'Let me check it for you on the Internet.'
F   'Oh, would you?'

Tell the students to look at the following replies to offers. Ask them to sort them into acceptances and refusals.

7 Look at the different replies to offers of help. Are the people accepting or refusing help?
Put a tick (✓) to show whether the answers are accepting or refusing.

Answers	Accepting	Refusing
'That's very kind of you, thanks.'	✓	
'It's okay, thanks. I can manage.'		✓
'Oh yes, please!'	✓	
'It's alright. Don't bother.'		✓
'I think I'm fine, thanks.'		✓
'Oh, would you? Brilliant!'	✓	
'That would be great. Thanks.'	✓	
'I'm alright actually. Thanks anyway.'		✓
'Thanks ever so much, but I think I can cope.'		✓

Tell the students to notice how polite all the replies are, regardless
of whether the people are accepting the offer or not.

Now tell the students to practise some of these expressions with
a partner. Tell them to use the pictures to help them. **(5 mins)**

**8 Work with your partner. Look at the pictures below.
Act out the situations by offering to help and accepting or refusing.**

Ask the students to work alone and match the questions in the first
column and the replies in the second column and decide where they
think the people are. **(5–10 mins)**

9 Match the offers and the replies. Where do you think these people are?

1 'Another sandwich?'

3 'Thanks for the offer,
but I'm quite happy
to do both.'

2 'Would you like
me to see you
across the road?'

8 'Mmm, thanks.
Black, please.'

3 'How about me
painting and
you papering?'

4 'Oh, would you? Thanks.
That'll save me
going to the office.'

4 'If you like, I can
give Mike the
report tomorrow.'

6 'No, it's alright, thanks.
It's not heavy.'

5 'Would you like
some roast chicken?'

1 'Thank you, but I'm full.'

6 'Let me take your
case for you.'

7 'Are you sure? Well, thanks a lot.
There is quite a pile.'

7 'I'll give you a hand
with those dishes.'

5 'Thanks all the same,
but I'm vegetarian.'

8 'How about a coffee?'

2 'That's very kind of you,
thanks. It's so busy.'

Tell the students to listen to the recording and check their answers.
Then play the tape again, asking the students to listen to the tone
and the intonation of the voices.

10 Listen to the recording to check your answers. 🔲 34

🔲 34

1

Male voice 'Another sandwich?'
Female voice 'Thank you, but I'm full.'

2

Female voice 1 'Would you like me to see you across the road?'
Female voice 2 'That's very kind of you, thanks. It's so busy.'

3

F 'How about me painting and you papering?'
M 'Thanks for the offer, but I'm quite happy to do both.'

4

Male voice 1 'If you like, I can give Mike the report tomorrow.'
Male voice 2 'Oh, would you? Thanks. That'll save me going to the office.'

5

F 'Would you like some roast chicken?'
M 'Thanks all the same, but I'm vegetarian.'

6

F1 'Let me take your case for you.'
F2 'No, it's alright, thanks. It's not heavy.'

7

M 'I'll give you a hand with those dishes.'
F 'Are you sure? Well, thanks a lot. There is quite a pile.'

8

F 'How about a coffee?'
M 'Mmm, thanks. Black, please.'

Ask the students to practise some more dialogues with a partner,
paying attention to the intonation and tone of their voices. Vary this
by putting up alternatives on the board. Walk around the class,
listening and advising.
asking for a drink
opening the door
driving or reading a map
answering a question
offering some strawberry ice-cream
putting on a coat
offering to do the cleaning
playing a game of tennis (5 mins)

---

11 Look at the suggestions your teacher writes on the board.
Roleplay the situations of offering/accepting/refusing with your partner.
Can you think of other situations?

5 Requesting and replying

Walk around the class, making some requests to the students (make sure some requests are to do things yourself and others are asking others to do something, eg, open window, clean the board, bring me a book). (2–3 mins)

Tell the students that when you ask for or request something, you usually do one of two things:
A ask for/to do something yourself.
B ask someone else to do something for you.

Ask the students if the requests are A or B. Play the recording. Get them to compare with a partner. Play again to check as a whole class. (5 mins)

1 **Listen to the recording. Are the people asking to do something themselves or for somebody else to do it for them?**
After listening, see if you and your partner agree. 🔊 35

🔊 35
1
Female voice 'Could you pass the salt, please?'
2
Male voice 'Lend me a hand with this video, would you?'
3
F 'Is it okay if I take a quick break?'
4
M 'Would you mind if I used your loo, please?'
5
F 'If you could show me how this program works, I'd be grateful.'

Ask the students to look at the pictures and say what the people are doing. Then get them to make requests to their partners, using the expressions. You might prefer to practise these expressions as a whole class first. (10 mins)

2 **Look at the pictures and ask your partner if you can do these things.**
These expressions might help you:

'Do you mind if I … ?'   'Is it okay/alright if I … ?'

'You don't mind if I … do you?'   'Can I/Could I … ?'

Next get them to look at the expressions used to introduce requests to get someone to do things for them. Get them to ask their partners to do the things in the pictures.

3 **Now ask your partner to do the things in activity 2.**
These expressions might help:

'Would/do you mind (+ gerund) … ?'

'Can you …, please?'

'You couldn't …, could you?'

Play the recording and ask them how similar their requests were. You can play it again for intonation practice, if you need to. (5–10 mins)

4 Listen to the recording. How similar were your requests? 📼 36

📼 36

1

Female voice 'Shall I answer the phone?'

2

Male voice 'You don't mind if I change channels, do you?'

3

F 'Is it okay if I shut the window?'

4

M 'I couldn't turn the music down a bit, could I?'

5

F 'Can I close the curtains, please?'

6

M 'Do you mind if I put the light on?'

7

F 'Would you mind closing the curtains, please?'

8

M 'Do you think we could switch channels, please?'

9

F 'Could you answer the phone?'

10

M 'Put the light on, would you?'

11

F 'Can you close the window, please?'

12

M 'You couldn't turn the music down a bit, could you?'

Ask the students to think of two requests (an A and a B) and get them to move around the room asking and answering as many people as they can. (5 mins)

5 What kinds of request can you make to the people in your classroom? Walk around, making as many requests as you can.

Ask the students to think about the different ways they might request things from people they know. (5–10 mins)

6 As in most languages, the way that you ask for something depends on who you are talking to.
Imagine that you need to borrow some money. Assume the following roles with your partner. How does your language change when talking to different people?

English teacher	best friend
boss	brother/sister
stranger at a party	

7 The tone of language you use also depends on the situation.
Rank the following requests from 1 (very informal) to 4 (very polite).

Requests	1 to 4
'Could you pass me that report, please?'	2
'I wonder if you'd mind passing me that report, please?'	4
'Hey, sling that report over, would you?'	1
'You couldn't pass me that report, could you?'	3

Ask the students to listen to the recording and to say how polite the requests are. Pause after each one. Discuss and stress that answers are not necessarily right or wrong, and meaning is influenced by the tone of the speaker. (5 mins)

8 Listen to the recording.
Who are the people and how polite are their requests? 🎧 37

People	Not very	Quite	Very	Extremely
family or friends	✓			
strangers who are travelling				✓
teacher and student			✓	
hairdresser and client		✓		

🎧 37

1
Male voice Get a move on, would you?'
Female voice 'Okay, okay. Keep your hair on.'
2
F 'I hope you don't mind me asking, but could you look after my bag
for a moment?'
M 'By all means.'
3
M 'Do you think you could go over my homework with me after class?'
F 'Sure. I'd be glad to.'
4
M 'Would you mind cutting it a bit shorter this time?
F 'Yes, of course. No problem.'

Divide the class into Group A and Group B.

Get the students to move around the class talking to as many people as they can. You can introduce further situations if they need more practice.

Get them to try using different levels of politeness with different people. They can then swap roles and move on to the next situation. (10–15 mins)

9   **Act out the following situations as roleplays, using different levels of politeness. Swap roles as you move on to the next partner.**

Phoning to change a hospital appointment

Student A: patient

Student B: hospital receptionist

Asking to leave class early

Student A: student

Student B: teacher

Borrowing a car

Student A: unreliable friend

Student B: friend

Getting a loan to start a business

Student A: customer

Student B: bank manager

Replying to requests

Get the students to match the requests and the replies. Then check through the replies of acceptance and refusal. (10 mins)

10 **Match the requests and the replies. Then practice the expressions here.**

1 'Can I borrow your dictionary?'

2 'Would you mind opening that window?'

3 'Lend me a couple of dollars, would you?'

4 'Could you post this for me on your way home?'

5 'I wonder if you could move your chair a bit. I can't see very well.'

2 'Of course. It is a bit stuffy in here.'

5 'Oh, sorry. There – is that better?'

4 'Sure. I'd be glad to drop it off for you.'

1 'By all means. It's on my desk.'

3 'So sorry I can't. I left my wallet at home.'

Agreeing	Refusing
'Sure.'	'I'm (so/very/awfully) sorry, but …'
'Of course.'	'I'm afraid I can't … '
'No problem.'	'I'd like/love to, but … '
'I'd be glad to.'	'I'd like to say yes, but …'
'By all means.'	'Another time I would, but … '
'Go ahead.'	

Activity 11 is an additional activity, 'the requesting game', which is a fun way to get the students to act out different situations.

11 The requesting game
Play this game with your partner. Toss a coin.
If it's heads, move forward 1 square and roleplay the situation.
If it's tails, move forward 2 squares.

Start

2   In a clothes shop. Ask to try on some jeans.

4   In class. You don't understand the lesson.

8   On a train. You need help with understanding the timetable.
    Ask the stranger opposite.

11 At a hotel. You want the key to your room.

14 At the bank. You need to change some money.

17 At a tourist office. You want a map of the town.

20 In a clothes shop. You want a smaller size in the sweater you like.

23 At a friend's house. You want to use the phone.

26 In a café. You want to sit nearer the window.

30 In a shoe shop. You want to try the same shoes in a different colour.

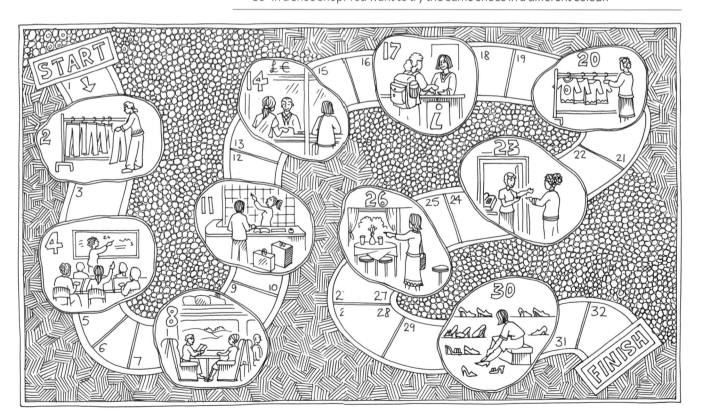

6 Describing people

Write up 'What does he or she look like?' on the board.

Draw three columns on the board. Write these column headings: 'hair', 'face', 'figure'.

Have ready a large, full-length, colour photograph. Ask the whole class to call out phrases to describe the person. Put the ideas in the appropriate column. (5 mins)

As a whole class, study the vocabulary used to describe physical appearance and illustrate any new words like 'spiky' on the board. (5 mins)

What does she look like?

Now ask the students to use this vocabulary and language structure to describe the girl in activity 1.

1   **Look at the picture of the girl. What words and phrases can we use to describe her physical appearance?**

She has short spiky hair.

She's got a squarish face.

She's about average height and weight.

She has her arms folded.

She's smiling./She looks happy.

She's wearing casual clothes and trainers.

Get the students to ask each other to describe their family, friends, teachers, neighbours. (5 mins)

2 **Ask people in your class to describe their family, friends, teachers and neighbours. Use these structures:**

Hair

'He/she's got	short	straight	
	blonde	shoulder-length	
	curly	dark	
	long	wavy	
	brown	spiky	
	grey		hair.'

'He's bald.'

Face

'He/she's got a/an	round		
	square		
	oval		
	long	face.'	
'He/she's got a	dark		
	fair		
	pale	complexion.'	

Figure

'He/she's	short.'
	quite thin.'
	extremely fat.'
	a bit plump.'
	very slim.'
	well-built.'
	average height.'
	really tall.'

Put the students in pairs. Student A shuts his or her eyes while student B describes someone in class, including what they're wearing today. Student A must guess who it is. Both students then discuss the accuracy of the description. (5 mins)

3 **Shut your eyes. Your partner will describe someone in class to you, including what they are wearing today. Can you guess who it is?**

Who is it?

Before class, prepare two colour magazine photographs of people for each student. Make sure the people in the pictures are all of a similar age and that there's a variety of physical difference. Cut them in half. Give four different halves to each student. Get the students to move around the class describing their halves in order to find the matches. They mustn't look at each other's pictures or describe the clothes. Move around, listening and monitoring. (5–10 mins)

4 **Your teacher will give you all four halves of photographs of different people. Other students will have the matching halves. Walk around the class, describing one or more of your photo halves. Don't describe their clothes. How many can you match up in 5 minutes?**

What's he or she like?

Show the whole class another set of photographs. Tell the class that this time you want them to imagine what each person's character is and what interests he or she might have. Write 'What's he or she like?' on the board. Brainstorm ideas and write them up. (2–5 mins)

Tell the students to listen to the recording and, looking at the pictures, decide who the people are talking about. (10 mins)

5 **Listen to the recording. Which person are they talking about?** 🔊 38

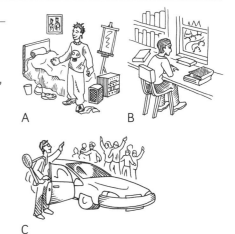

🔊 38

1

Male voice 'So, what's Geoff like?'
Female voice 'Well, he's a quiet sort of bloke. He enjoys his own company, quite relaxed.'
M 'What sort of age is he?'
F 'Oh, late 30s, I should guess.'
M 'And what's he interested in?'
F 'He's a big reader. And he loves his garden too.' B
2
F **'Do you know Matt very well?'**
M 'Fairly well. We shared an office for a year.'
F **'What's he like?'**
M 'He's very outgoing, you know, sociable…'
F **'He sounds great!'**
M 'There is another side to him, though. He can be a bit selfish and vain.'
F **'Well, he is very good-looking. He's sporty too, isn't he?'**
M 'Yes, he plays a lot of tennis and he's mad about sports cars.' C

3
Female voice 1 'What's Damian like these days?'
Female voice 2 'He's crazier than ever. But he's a lot less moody than he used to be.'
F1 'Is he still listening to all that weird music?'
F2 'Yes, and he's taken up painting too.'
F1 'Oh no! I wonder what his room looks like…' A

Work through the vocabulary items with the whole class, eliciting the name of a famous person, either from fiction or real-life, to go with each of the character traits.

6 **Look at some vocabulary that is helpful when describing a person's character:**

quiet, shy, an introvert, unsociable

friendly, easy-going, sociable, outgoing, an extrovert, a good mixer

kind, helpful, thoughtful, good company , pleasant, tolerant

moody, bad-tempered, unkind, selfish, lazy

he/she likes/loves/enjoys/is mad about …

Put the class into groups. Each person describes another student's character. The rest of the group must guess who it is. (5–10 mins)

7 Describing things and places

Draw the shapes in activity 1 on the board. Ask for the nouns and adjectives. Practise the contrast in pronunciation, eg, 'rectangle/rectangular'. Then brainstorm objects which have these shapes. (5–10 mins)

1 Match the pictures and the correct nouns and adjectives.

diamond/ diamond-shaped	star/ star-shaped	circle/ circular/round	rectangle/ rectangular
triangle/ triangular	crescent/ crescent-shaped	semi-circle/ semi-circular	heart/ heart-shaped
square	oval	T-shape/d	L-shape/d

star   rectangle   heart   oval

diamond   L-shape   circle   semi-circle

square   triangle   crescent   T-shape

Get the students to match the vocabulary with the pictures. Practise the pronunciation as a whole class. (5 mins)

2 Match the pictures and the lines and patterns.

straight/ horizontal	curved	vertical	diagonal
flowered	wavy	sloping	parallel
striped	spotted	checked	plain

striped   wavy   sloping   plain

diagonal   straight   spotted   vertical

flowered   curved   parallel   checked

Working in pairs, Student A describes one of the pictures in activity 3 using the given vocabulary and Student B guesses which picture it is. Students then swap. (5–10 mins)

3 Describe the pictures.

Then play the recording. Ask how similar their descriptions are.

4 Listen to the recording. How similar are your descriptions? 🔊 39

🔊 39

1
Male voice 'I bought her a lovely little heart-shaped locket made of gold.'

2
Female voice 'It's a square, wooden table with curved legs.'
3
M 'Mine's the blue-and-white striped mug.'

4
F 'There were two people walking up the sloping path.'
5
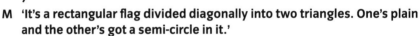
M 'I've got a new spotted T-shirt.'
6
F 'The cliff's absolutely vertical.'
7
M 'It's a rectangular flag divided diagonally into two triangles. One's plain and the other's got a semi-circle in it.'
8
F 'The picture's got wavy lines.'

The five senses

With the whole class, write the five senses on the board. Take some objects out of your bag (eg, a CD, a piece of material, a flower, a bar of soap, a picture, an apple). Ask which sense is most necessary to appreciate the objects. (5 mins)

Get the students in their pairs to discuss which senses are most important for the jobs in the pictures in activity 5. (5–10 mins)

5 Which of the five senses – sight, sound, taste, smell and touch – is the most vital for each of these occupations? Why?

sight

taste

smell

sound

Discuss feedback with the whole class. Are there any disagreements?

Looks, seems, appears, looks like

Study the language suggested by the four pictures in activity 6 with the class. (5–10 mins)

sight/touch   sight

6 Match the pictures and the descriptions of the people.

'She looks happy.'

'He seems miserable.'

'He appears to be hypnotised.'

'She looks like a pop star.' (resembles)

Get the students to work in pairs and give each one a photo of a person. Ask the students to describe the person in their photo to their partner and to ask the partner if they agree. They must use the language they have just studied. (5–10 mins)

7 Look at the photos your teacher gives you. How do the people look, seem or appear?

hypnotised

looks like a pop star

happy

miserable

Study the expressions to describe sound and then play the recording, pausing after each sound. Get the students to discuss with their partners what the noises sound like and to write them down. (10 mins)

Sound

8   **Listen to the recording. What are the sounds like? Discuss them with your partner.** 🔊 40
Here are some phrases you could use:

'It sounds like footsteps.' (sound + like + noun)

'The music sounds lively.' (sound + adjective)

🔊 40
Sounds of:
1
washing up
2
footsteps
3
creaking door
4
drum roll
5
chalk squeaking on board
6
computer printing
7
opening a bottle of fizzy cola

Play the recording again and confirm the answers with the class.

Touch

Study the structures 'feel like' with a noun and 'feel' with an adjective. (2–5 mins)

Ask the students to look at the pictures and to describe what the different items feel like to a partner. Move around the class, monitoring and supplying vocabulary. (5 mins)

9 **What do these things feel like? Describe them using phrases such as:**

'It feels like fur.' (feel + like + noun)

'They feel quite rough.' (feel + adjective)

Work with the whole class. Blindfold a student. Give him or her an object to feel and describe, and guess its identity. If some students are shy, they can work in pairs.

Smell

Study the structures describing the sense of smell. (5 mins)

This is an optional activity, depending on the class and the accessibility of props. (15–20 mins)

Tell the students to blindfold their partners, and test them with a number of smells. Ask them to describe them! Can they guess all of them?

10 **Blindfold your partner and test him or her with a number of smells (different herbs, cocoa, coffee, fruits, vegetables, perfumes, furniture polish, etc). What do each of the items smell like?**
Do any of them smell like something else?
How many can you guess correctly?
You can use these phrases to talk about smell:

'My fingers smell of garlic.' (smell + of = an exact smell)

'This flower smells like chocolate.' (smell + like = reminds me of)

Taste

Study the structures describing the sense of taste. (5 mins)

This is an optional activity, depending on the class and the accessibility of props.

Get the students, working in pairs, to blindfold their partners. They then taste a number of foods (eg, yogurt, banana, orange, lemon, salt, honey, onion, crisps). Ask them to describe the tastes! Can they guess all of them? (15–20 mins)

11 Practise describing different kinds of food and drink. Use these phrases:

'It tastes really creamy.' (taste + adjective)

'This orange tastes a bit sour.'

'This biscuit tastes of almonds.' (taste + of = an exact taste)

'This soup tastes like mud!' (taste + like = reminds me of)

Describing places

Ask the students to listen to the recording and to discuss in small groups which places are being described. (5–10 mins)

12 Listen to the recording. Which places do you think are being described? Why? Discuss your ideas in small groups. 🔊 41

🔊 41

1

Male voice 'It's situated on the High Street right next to Barclays Bank. It's on two floors – very light and airy with a nice relaxed atmosphere. There are about 20 tables, I should think – it's self-service, but there's never much of a queue. I like it because it's quite cheap and they have the daily papers which you can borrow.'

2

Female voice 'It's very near the station. It's really badly designed because you've got to go through one room to get to another and the toilet is actually in the bathroom, which I hate. The reasons I dislike it so much are the damp and the constant noise of the trains.'

3

Male voice 2 'You'll find it at the bottom end of town. It looks really small from the outside but when you go in, it's like a castle or something. It's got three floors. The ground floor starts with the really early history of the town. Then you gradually move through the centuries as you make your way upstairs. The reason I like it so much is because you can actually touch a lot of the exhibits – you know, the things on show. It's great for children. You can really learn such a lot there.'

Study the language for describing places with the whole class.

Get the students to think of some places they know well and to describe their favourite and least favourite example. Get the students to change partners if you feel it's necessary. (20–30 mins)

13 Look at the types of places below. Think of examples of each that you know well.

Working in pairs, describe your most and least favourite example of each one. Which place would you most and least like to see? Use some of the ideas and expressions that follow to help you.

a house

a museum

a restaurant

a shop

a holiday resort

Location

'It's situated ...'

'It's very near ...'

'It's not far from ...'

'You'll find it ...'

'It's right next to ....'

Interior design

'It's well/badly designed.'

'It's on one/two floors.'

'When you go in, you'll see ...'

'It's got two bedrooms/a lot of space/a lot of light.'

Positives

'What I like about the place is …'

'Most of all, I like it because …'

'The reason I like it so much is because …'

Negatives

'I dislike it mainly because …'

'What I really hate about it is …'

'The thing I don't like is …'

Recommending

'You'd love it because …'

'You really ought to go there because …'

I'm sure you'd like it because …'

8 Expressing opinions

Tell the students they are going to listen to some people talking. Get them to try to work out what the people on the recording are talking about (a film, camping, trains). Pause after each dialogue and get them to discuss with a partner. Then play the recording again and confirm as a whole class. (5–10 mins)

1 **Listen to the recording. What do you think the people are asking about? Ask your partner. Do you agree?** 🔲 42

🔲 42

1

Male voice 'So what did you think of the ……, then?'
Female voice 'Well, if you ask me, it was a bit disappointing.'

M 'Really? In what way?'
F   'Hm… well, the special effects were okay, but the story line was a bit thin and the ending was absolutely awful.'

2

F 'How do you feel about going …… ?'
M 'You must be joking! Definitely not!'

F 'Why do you say that?'
M 'I hate insects, I don't like trying to cook when it's pouring with rain and I like to sleep in a comfortable bed if I'm going on holiday.'

3

M 'What's your opinion of the …… in this country?'
F   'I'm very impressed by them. Especially compared with my country.'

M 'Oh, why's that?'
F   'Well, for a start, they're so punctual here. At home they're never on time. And the platforms and waiting rooms are so clean…'

Study the structures for asking for and giving opinions as a whole class. (15 mins)

2 **Look at the different ways of asking for and giving an opinion.**

Asking

'What do/did you think of …?' (the concert, my new sofa, that teacher, etc)

'How do you feel about …?' (this idea, doing something, etc)

'What's your feeling about …?' (this idea, doing something, etc)

'What's your opinion of …?' (a political party, the economic situation, the news, etc)

Answering

'I think (+ statement).'

'I believe (+ statement).'

'In my opinion (+ statement).'

'In my view (+ statement).'

Informal

'If you ask me, …'

'Do you want to know what I think? Well, …'

'To be (quite) honest with you, I think …'

Formal

'As far as I'm concerned, …'

'From my point of view, …'

Get the students to debate topics about which they have opinions and feelings, the stronger the better. Prepare by writing topics on slips of paper and putting the slips into a bag. Include some topics you've not yet discussed in class.There should be enough for one or two per student. Get the students into small groups. Each person picks one of the slips out of the bag.

In their groups they ask for and give opinions on the topics, keeping their comments to one or two sentences each. Encourage them to use the expressions you have just studied.

Here are some ideas for topics:
1 Your English class
2 My hairstyle
3 A film you've seen
4 A particular book
5 Vegetarianism
6 Body piercing
7 Shopping on the Internet
8 Mobile phones (20–30 mins)

Agreeing and disagreeing

As a whole class, look at the expressions for agreeing and disagreeing.
Then in pairs, the students decide which are used when agreeing or
disagreeing and which are formal or informal.
Check and confirm answers as a whole class. (10–15 mins)

3   Which of these expressions show that you agree and which
show that you disagree? Which are formal and which informal?
Put a tick in the column you think is correct and then compare
your list with your partner.

Expressions	Agree	Disagree	Formal	Informal
'What?!'		✓		✓
'Oh, absolutely.'	✓		✓	
'You've got to be joking.'		✓		✓
'I couldn't agree more.'	✓		✓	
'Come off it!'		✓		✓
'I'm with you there.'	✓			✓
'I agree entirely.'	✓		✓	
'You can't be serious!'		✓		✓
'I'm afraid I think you're wrong.'		✓	✓	
'But that's total rubbish.'		✓		✓
'You're quite right.'	✓		✓	
'You've got a point there.'	✓			✓
'How can you say that?'		✓		✓
'I agree up to a point.'	✓		✓	

Look at the following statements as a whole class. Put the students into pairs. Ask the students to respond to the statements by using some of the expressions you have studied. Tell them to think about how formally and politely they reply. Get them to try different levels of formality with different topics. (15–30 mins)

4 **Look at these statements. What are your views?**

Statements	Agree	Disagree
'There shouldn't be any experiments on animals.'		
'All pop music is rubbish.'		
'What young people need is military service.'		
'Computers will kill off books eventually.'		
'Everyone should learn at least one foreign language.'		
'This town's just great for young people.'		
'Being famous would be awful.'		

Feedback at the end of the session by asking which views the students found most surprising.

Test practice

The organisation of the test practice is a matter for your judgement in the particular teaching situation you are in. With larger classes, it can be difficult to use the practice test as an activity in class time. You can ask the students to practise in pairs, with one adopting the role of interlocutor, but if it is possible to conduct the practice exercise (and at some stage a full practice test) yourself or have a fellow teacher do so, it will be valuable test preparation.

(This type of task would normally take only a few minutes in the test itself and one of the test skills to cultivate is a fluent exchange of information/comment in a short time.)

Test practice – Achiever

The following situations are similar to those you will be expected to act out with the interlocutor in Part 2 of the Spoken ESOL test at the Achiever level.
For the first two situations, the interlocutor will start by saying:
'… first of all I'm going to read two situations and I want you to respond.'
In each situation you will be expected to speak at least twice.
Responding
'I'm a new student in your English class. I start.
"Which books do we need?"'

'We're friends. I start.
"Do you want to go to the beach on Saturday?"'

'I'm your teacher. I start.
"I haven't had your homework. Where is it?"'

'I'm your friend. I start.
"You don't look very well. What's the matter?"'

'I work in a shoe shop. I start.
"Good morning. Can I help you?"'

'You're a guest in my house. I start.
"What would you like to drink?"'

For the second two situations, the interlocutor will start by saying:
'… now I'm going to read two more situations and I want you to start.'
In each situation you will be expected to speak at least twice.
Starting
'I'm your teacher. You don't know the word "floor". Ask me. You start.'

'I'm your friend. Invite me to your barbecue. You start.'

'I sell cinema tickets. You want to buy some. You start.'

'I'm a stranger. You want to find a bank. You start.'

'It's my birthday. You start.'

'I'm a waiter. Your meal isn't very good. You start.'

Test practice – Communicator

The following situations are similar to those you will be expected to act out with the interlocutor in Part 2 of the Spoken ESOL test at the Communicator level.
For the first two situations, the interlocutor will start by saying:
'… first of all I'm going to read two situations and I want you to respond.'
In each situation you will be expected to speak at least twice.
Responding
'I'm your friend. I start.
"I really need to get fit. What do you suggest?"'

'I'm your boss at work.
"I wonder if you'd mind working late tonight?"'

'I'm your neighbour.
"I'm afraid you're parking in my parking space."'

'I'm your doctor.
"So what seems to be the problem?"'

'I'm your English teacher.
"Which area of English do you think you need more practice in and why?"'

'I'm a stranger in your town.
"Excuse me, but is there a decent hotel round here?"'

For the second two situations, the interlocutor will start by saying:
'… now I'm going to read two more situations and I want you to start.'
In each situation you will be expected to speak at least twice.
Starting
'You're in a music shop. You want to buy a CD. You start.'

'I'm your friend. Persuade me to take up running with you. You start.'

'I'm your friend. I look worried. You start.'

'I work in a clothes shop. The jeans you bought are faulty. You start.'

'I'm your teacher. You need to leave class early. You start.'

'You're going on holiday. You need someone to look after your pets. You start.'

Introduction to Part 3

In Part 3 of the book the emphasis is on exchanging information and opinions by asking and answering questions, and on making choices, arrangements and plans. Likewise, in Part 3 of the Spoken ESOL test, the candidate exchanges information with the interlocutor.

At the Achiever level, the candidate and the interlocutor will both have the same test sheet. They will carry out a joint task, such as choosing a present for a friend. There will be around six pictures to serve as prompts – for example, a book, chocolates, a plant, etc. The candidate will exchange information and views with the interlocutor to evaluate the choices and reach a joint decision.

At the Communicator level, the candidate and interlocutor will have different test sheets. They might, for example, each have their diary for the coming week, and want to make plans to see a film together. They will consult their diaries and exchange information in order to find a day and time that both are free – and they might want to choose a film and make other arrangements such as deciding where to meet.

To do well in this part of the exam, the candidate must both ask and answer questions. There is no specific mark for task achievement, however, the more items candidates discuss, the more likely they are to demonstrate an appropriate range of language. The exercises encourage students to practise the exchange of information and opinions, and the recordings that support each unit give models of language for students to follow. Turn-taking is very much a feature of Part 3 of the test, and students can usefully practise interrupting, asking for and giving clarification, and referring directly to what has been said by a partner in the interaction.

It is in the nature of information-exchange tasks that the interaction can take unexpected directions. Encourage your students to use the language strategies which make interaction seem natural: repeating what a partner has said, often in a rising tone to suggest disagreement; filling pauses with such language items as 'Well…' 'Let me see…' 'Could it be…'.

3

Part 3 Exchanging information and opinions

We often talk with other people to find out things that we don't know. We may have some information, but need to fill in some gaps. We may want to plan an activity that involves other people or compare our views with those of a workmate. Exchanging information can be important in both our work and social lives. The units that follow are designed to build skills in exchanging information and opinions.

In Part 3 of the Spoken ESOL test you need to use English in order to give and receive information to carry out a specific task. The units that follow will give you practice. In each unit there are games and activities to help you with exchanging information, problem-solving, constructive discussion and task achievement.

Tips from the examiners

For Part 3 of the exam, the candidate and the interlocutor have separate test sheets. At the Achiever level there will be pictures to help you, but at the Communicator level the information will mainly be written. Here are some examples of the kinds of task you and the interlocutor may be asked to do together:
– choose a gift
– plan a party
– compare diaries to arrange an evening out
– put things in a particular order (ranking) and explain why.
Try to make your exchanges as natural and fluent as possible. Remember, there usually isn't a right answer in Part 3, and you don't always have to finish the task.

1 Choosing the best and the worst

Tell the students they are going to listen to a recording of two people talking about different places to stay on holiday. Ask them to look at the questions. Tell them to listen and answer the questions. Get them to discuss their answers with a partner. Then play a second time, pausing the recording and checking their answers. (5 mins)

1 Listen to the recording.
Alan and Cristina are talking about different places to stay on holiday. Answer the questions as you listen and compare your answers with your partner. Listen again to check them. ▢▢ 43

Why doesn't Alan like camping? raining, leaky tent, couldnt cook, mosquitoes

What does Cristina think is good about camping? independence, cheap

Why does Alan enjoy staying in a hotel? comfort, everything done for you

Why doesn't Cristina like hotels? too formal, smart

What does Cristina like about staying in a self-catering apartment?
comfortable, freedom

▢▢ 43

Alan 'Hi, Cristina. I'm just looking at these holiday magazines and deciding where to go this year – there's so much choice…'

Cristina 'Mmm, I know what you mean. What kind of holiday are you thinking of – are you going camping again like last year?'

A 'No, I'm not – never again! It was terrible – it rained every night and the tent leaked, I couldn't cook anything properly and the mosquitoes nearly drove us crazy…'

C (laughing) 'Oh dear, poor you! I really like camping myself – I love being able to do whatever I like – you know, be really independent. And it's a very cheap kind of holiday too…'

A 'Well, yes, I suppose that's true … but for me, nothing beats the comfort of being looked after in a really nice hotel, you know, having everything done for you, your food cooked, your bed made, and…'

C (laughing) 'Alan, you lazy thing … I think some hotels can be a bit formal, oh, you know, having to look smart when you go to dinner and everything. No, for me, the best place to stay is in a self-catering apartment. You can be comfortable and free at the same time…'

Ask the students to look at the different places to stay on holiday. Check that they know the vocabulary. Ask them, in their pairs, to discuss what would be good or bad about staying in these different places. Then ask them to say which they like the most and the least. Ask them to try to persuade their partners to agree with them. Walk around and monitor. Write any useful vocabulary which arises (eg, 'lonely', 'noisy', 'comfortable') on the board. (5 mins)

2 Look at these different places to stay on holiday.
What would be good or bad about staying in each one?
Discuss your ideas with a partner and decide which you'd like
best and which you'd like least.
Try to persuade your partner to agree with you.

Tell the students they are going to listen to some conversations about
people's likes and dislikes. Ask them to listen for and make notes of the
phrases that the people use to show that they like or dislike something.
Get them to compare with a partner. Then play the tape again. Ask the
students to call out the helpful phrases. Write them on the board.
Then get them to listen once again and practise. (5 mins)

3 Listen to the four conversations – which phrases help you
to understand what the speakers like or don't like?
Make a note of them and then compare your notes with your partner.
Listen again and practise. 📼 44

_____

_____

_____

_____

📼 44
1
M **'What kind of music do you listen to, to relax, Martina? Classical?'**
F 'Oh no. I prefer listening to jazz when I want to relax.'
2
F **'Would you like orange juice to drink with your curry?'**
M 'I'd rather have some water, please, if you don't mind.'
3
M **'What did you think of the art exhibition, Karen? Did you like it?'**
F 'I quite liked it. My favourite painting was the one of the garden. I thought the worst
one was that huge painting of the horse … it was really terrible…'
4
F **'So let's decide which colour to paint the kitchen. Here's the book with the
choice of colours…'**
M 'Hm … Well, I think the best one is this dark blue – it's called "Deep Sea"…'
F **'Oh, I wouldn't choose that – it's much too dark. I like this one the most –
"Apple Green". Do you like it?'**
M 'Oh no! That's my least favourite of all … it's awful.'
F **'Oh dear. Maybe we'd better just leave it as it is…'**

Ask the students to look at the illustrations of different kinds of film.
Ask them to give titles to the films and then say what the genre is, eg,
'The Thing That Appeared in the Night' – 'Horror'. Write the students'
suggestions and genre names on the board, eg, Horror/Western/Action/
Science-Fiction/Cartoon/Romance/Period drama/Comedy (5–10 mins)

Put the students in small groups. Ask them to discuss what they like and dislike about the different kinds of film. Tell them to think of examples of each kind of film. Are there any other genres they like? Ask them to say which they like the most and the least. Ask them to use some of the phrases they heard on the recording (still on the board). (5–10 mins)

4   **Look at these different kinds of film.**

Discuss what you like and dislike about these different kinds of film. Can you think of examples of each sort of film? Which do you like the most and the least? Do you agree with each other?
Try to use some of the phrases you heard on the recording.

Now tell the students they are going to imagine that their teacher is leaving. Ask them to work in pairs to look at the presents and to discuss if they are suitable or unsuitable. Get them to say why. Then ask them to choose the most and the least suitable present. See how many pairs agree. (5 mins)

5   **Imagine that your English teacher is leaving.**
You and your partner want to buy him or her a present.
Discuss the presents below with your partner and decide which would be the most and the least suitable present for your teacher.

2 Planning and arranging

Tell the students they are going to hear two friends planning what to do on Saturday night. You are going to pause the recording in various places and get the students to predict what the friends will say next. This will engage them in the process and language of planning and arranging. The tapescript is marked at appropriate places to pause. Once about five or six guesses have been made, play the recording until the next pause. (5 mins)

1 **Listen to the recording.**
  Two friends are planning what to do on Saturday night.
  Your teacher will pause the dialogue in certain places – can you predict what comes next? 📼 45

📼 45

Female voice '**Hi, Mark. I've got Saturday night off this week.**'
Male voice 'Hey, that's great. Why don't we (pause) do something?'
F '**Okay, what do you fancy doing?**'
M 'How about (pause) a film?'
F '**Hm, I'm not sure. I had a look at what's on this week, but nothing really grabbed me…**'
M 'Well, we could always (pause) go out for a meal. There's a new Moroccan restaurant opened on The Green. It looks quite good.'
F '**Sorry, but I'm on a bit of a diet this week – just fruit and raw vegetables for five days.**'
M 'Oh, right! Unless you'd like to come along and watch me eat? No, sorry, only joking.'
F '**I tell you what. There's that band that used to play (pause) at college, um … what were they called?**'
M 'White (pause) Light?'
F '**Yeah, that's right. Well, they're playing a free concert in the park on Saturday night. I wouldn't mind going, actually. What about you?**'
M 'Okay. Why (pause) not? What time do they start?'
F '**Eight-thirty, I think.**'
M 'Right. Why don't I (pause) pick you up at eight?'
F '**Cool.**'

Write the word 'Tonight' on the board. Ask two or three students what they are doing tonight. Ask how you began the question. Elicit 'What are you doing …?' and write it up. Get the class to brainstorm other times: eg, 'next Monday', 'on Sunday', 'at the weekend', 'next year', 'at six o'clock'. (5 mins)

Tell the students to ask their partners what they are doing at these times. You can ask one or two students what the most exciting plans are, as class feedback.

Tell the students that an English visitor is coming to your school/college to speak to your English class. In pairs, the students have to make all the arrangements for the visit. (5–10 mins)

Tell the pairs of students that they both have different ideas about the following points. They must discuss their different ideas and try to reach agreement. While the students are exchanging ideas, go round the class monitoring and assisting where necessary. **(5 mins)**

2   **An English visitor is coming to your school or college to speak to your English class.**
You and your partner are making all the arrangements, but you both have different ideas about the following points.
Discuss your ideas and try to reach agreement.

When?

What should the visitor talk about?

Where and how long for?

Accommodation?

Dinner – where?

At the end of the session, elicit some feedback on the easiest things to agree about and the most difficult.

Write the words 'Big Surf Bay' on the board. Draw a large curling wave and a pin-man lying under a palm tree. Get the students to brainstorm things they might need to plan if they were going on holiday. **(2–5 mins)**

Now ask the students to work with a different partner. Tell them that they are planning a week's holiday at Big Surf Bay. **(5–10 mins)**

3   **You and your partner are planning a week's holiday at Big Surf Bay. Big Surf Bay is a beach resort with a luxury hotel, several small hotels, self-catering accommodation and a campsite. It is quite a lively resort with several nightclubs, a cinema, and a lot of small beachfront restaurants, which range from Chinese take-aways to burger bars, local family-run restaurants and pizzerias. Big Surf Bay can be reached from the airport by hire car, by ferry or by bus. Nearby mountains offer hiking and mountaineering activities, while the beach offers all kinds of water sports, such as jet-skis, pedal boats and windsurfing. Excursions from the resort include a bus trip to the old town of Rodas and speedboat trips to the harbour on the other side of the bay.**
Try to plan your trip according to your budget, likes and dislikes, and reach agreement on all the points listed.
When you've finished, tell another pair of students what you've decided and why.

Where to stay

How to travel

What to do (daytime)

What to do (night-time)

Where to eat

What to take

Ask the students to try to reach agreement on the points. When they have finished, they should tell another pair what they've decided and why. (3 mins)

Let's have a party!

Ask the students to read the questions before listening to the recording of some people planning a party. (5–10 mins)

4 Listen to the recording. Can you answer the following questions? Discuss your ideas with your partner. 46

Where are they having the party? back room/garden at the Internet café

Why are they having it? Sarah's 18th birthday

How many people are coming? 70–90

What kind of food are they having? cold buffet, cake and desserts

Who's doing the catering? guests bringing buffet, café doing cake and desserts

Why aren't they inviting Derek? has quarrelled with Sarah

Are they having live music? no

46

Male voice 1 'Right. Are we all agreed that Sarah mustn't know anything about this party? It's got to be a complete surprise, hasn't it?'

All 'Yes.' 'Oh, yes.' 'Absolutely.'

Female voice 1 'And it's her 18th birthday, isn't it?'

Male voice 1 'That's right. So it ought to be really special.'

Female voice 2 'Well, we've decided when, but not where. What does everyone think?'

Male voice 2 'Well, the Royal Hotel's fantastic. My parents had their wedding anniversary there.'

M1 'But that's going to be way too expensive to hire, isn't it?

F1 'I think it'd be too formal too – you know, too posh. Why don't we rent the back room at the Internet Café? It's cheap and it opens onto the garden at the back.'

All 'Great idea.' 'Oh, yeah.'

M1 'Okay then. It's quite big, isn't it? I should think it would hold 100 people, don't you?'

F1 'Oh, yes, easily. How many people are you actually inviting?'

F2 'Between 70 and 90.'

M2 'It's got a very good sound system and I don't think we need a live band, do you?'

M1 'No, no. It's too expensive and, anyway, Ricky can be the DJ. He's brilliant at it.'

F1 'Yes. Sarah'd love that too. So what about the food? Shall we ask the café to do the food or shall we do it ourselves?'

F2 'Why don't we ask the café to make the cake and the desserts, and everyone who's invited can bring something for a cold buffet. You know, salads, cold meats, crisps, that kind of thing.'

M1 **'Another brilliant idea. Everyone agree?'**

All *'Yes.' 'Excellent.'*

F1 'And how about Derek? Should we ask him to come?'

M2 **'Definitely not. Sarah still doesn't believe that girl she saw him with in the park was his long lost sister from Australia. We don't want any kind of quarrel to spoil what's going to be the best party ever … now, do we?'**

Play the recording once and then get the students to discuss their answers in small groups. Play the recording a second time and pause it in the appropriate places to confirm the answers. This is a good time to do some work on rising and falling tag-ends. You can play the recording a third time, asking students to identify the tags and practise them. (5 mins)

Put the students in groups. Ask the students individually to rank the following things in order of importance. Then get them to discuss their choices in groups. (15–30 mins)

5 **What makes a good party? Put the following things in order of importance when you are planning a party from 1 (most important) to 10 (least important).**

Factors	1 to 10
Place	
Music	
Weather	
Mix of people	
Atmosphere	
Lighting	
Food and drink	
Reason for the party	
Meeting someone special	
Dancing	

Tell the students that they've got a budget of £200 for a class party. In groups, they must plan the party, covering all the above points and staying within the budget. Each group briefly presents their plan to the rest of the class. Ask them to vote on which plan sounds the best.

6 **You've got a budget of £200 to organise an end-of-term party for your class. In groups, plan the party covering all the above points. Then choose a member of your group to present briefly your plans to the rest of the class.**

3 Discussing and deciding
Survival!

Tell the students to listen to the recording. It describes a hot-air balloon taking off – it's blown off course – next day it floats aimlessly – an albatross punctures the balloon – the balloon drops into ocean – there is a desert island in the distance (trees, fruit, water, coral reef). After listening to the recording, elicit the story from the students, by asking questions. (5–10 mins)

1   Listen to the recording. What's happening? 🔊 47

🔊 47

Male voice 1 'Come on, everyone. Into the basket. That's it. Mind that rope. Careful getting in.'

Female voice 1 'I'm so excited. This is my first time ever in a hot-air balloon. Such a lovely day too!'

Female voice 2 'I know. But I'm a bit scared. You know, being up so high with no real control of where we're going.'

Male voice 2 'Don't you worry about a thing. Just sit back and enjoy it. We've got the most experienced balloonist in the country with us today.'

M1 'Right, everyone, this is it. Lift-off.'

(Noise of whooshing hot air and cries from everyone. Fade out.)

F1 'It's fantastic. Everything is so clear and yet it just looks like a toy town.'

M2 'Oh, look, we're coming to the coast.'

F2 'It's getting quite windy, too, isn't it?'

M1 'Okay, everyone, hold tight. I think I might need your help in a minute …

(Fade out. Sound of water and sea birds.)

F2 'We've been up here for over 24 hours.'

F1 'Thank goodness we brought food and drink with us.'

M2 'Where exactly are we, Mike?'

M1 'Hm, good question. We're over the ocean, but where exactly I'm not…'

F2 'Watch out! Look! That absolutely enormous bird with an even more enormous beak is heading right for us!'

(Sound of balloon being punctured)

F1 'Oh, good grief. It's punctured the balloon…'

*(Terrible hissing sound. Cries of 'Help', 'We're going down', etc.
Sound of water and sea birds.)*

M1 'Well, I told you the trip would be exciting!'

F1 'But what are we going to do?'

M2 'Look! In the distance! A desert island! With trees and mountains.'

F2 'We could paddle the basket towards it …'

M1 'But it's too heavy. Look! We're sinking! We need to make the basket lighter.'

F1 'And you know what that means, don't you…?'

Now tell the students that they are the balloon passengers and that the balloon basket is sinking and three people must be thrown overboard for the rest to get to the island. Put the names of a variety of professions and jobs into a hat or box, folded up, and go round the class for the students to pick out their job, eg, doctor, water diviner, fisherman, policeman, teacher, musician, farmer, psychiatrist, cook, clown, judge, tailor, philosopher, storyteller, engineer, carpenter, sailor.

Now the students must work individually to prepare a speech of no longer than two minutes each (one minute if you have a big class) in which they must say why they are necessary for life on the island. Tell them they each have a small bag with the tools of their trade. Encourage them to ask for vocabulary to help them They have about five minutes to prepare. In this time you write all the jobs in a list on the board. This is good practice for developing an argument.

Then, picking out the names at random, you ask each student to stand and give their defence, timing and stopping them.

If there is time, you can have an open question-and-answer session before asking the whole class to write the names of the three least necessary passengers on a piece of paper and put them into the hat. You then take out the votes and put a tick next to those jobs which have been voted out. The three most voted for are thrown overboard! (30–40 mins)

2 **You are one of the passengers in the balloon.**
   You have about 5 minutes to prepare your defence.
   Why are you necessary for survival on the island?
   You are going to talk for 1 or 2 minutes to the rest of the class,
   telling them why you should not be thrown overboard.
   You can make notes but don't write out the whole speech.

Write up £250 (or equivalent currency) on the board. Ask the students what they would buy or do with this money, if you gave it to them now. Brainstorm for ideas. Write a few of the ideas up. (5 mins)

Put the class into small groups. Tell them to imagine that their class has £250 remaining from the class budget. It is up to the group to decide how to spend the money, but it must be a democratic process and should benefit everyone. Ask them to write down all the ideas without discussing them. Then, in their groups, decide on the one best idea. Finally one person from each group should make a brief argument for its choice and the whole class decides the overall winner. (15–30 mins)

3   Imagine that your English class has £250 remaining from its budget.
    It is up to all of you to decide how to spend the money, but it must
    be a democratic process and should benefit you all.
    First write down all the ideas you have without discussing them.
    Then, in your groups, decide on the one best idea.
    Finally one person from each group should make a brief argument
    for its choice so that the whole class can decide what to choose.

Tell the students to listen to the recording. Ask them to listen for phrases
which are:
used to introduce someone's idea
used to persuade someone else
used to show something's been decided.   (10 mins)

4   **Listen to the recording.**
    Note down the phrases that function in the ways listed below. 📼 48

Phrases used to introduce someone's idea	Phrases used to persuade someone else	Phrases used to show something's been decided
personally, I'd much rather	you've got to admit	are we all agreed
from my point of view	you can't argue with	that settles it

📼 48

**Female voice 1 'So we've got to decide whether to go camping or stay in a
    little hotel. What do you all think?'**
**Female voice 2 'Well, personally, I'd much rather go camping. You know,
    sitting out under the stars, telling stories…'**
Male voice 1 'Getting bitten to death by mosquitoes…'
F1 'Oh, come on – be a bit more romantic, for goodness' sake.'
Male voice 2 'Romantic! From my point of view, there is absolutely nothing at all
    romantic about eating burnt sausages out in the rain.'
M1 'And you've got to admit that a small comfortable hotel with a nice little restaurant…'
F1 '…would not be very exciting.'
**F2 'I really think we need to do something different this year and camping
    in the mountains…'**
M2 '…is not my idea of relaxation, I'm afraid.'
F1 'In my opinion, we ought to be democratic about this.'
**F2 'Good idea! You can't argue with spending one week camping and
    one week at a hotel.'**
M1 'We'll need it just to recover!'
F1 'So are we all agreed?'
All 'Yes, okay.' 'Oh, alright.'
M2 'Well, that settles it then.
F2 'Or perhaps a walking holiday instead…?'
All (Groans)

After playing the recording once, ask for the phrases and write them
in one of the three columns on the board. Play the recording again,
pausing at each phrase and studying/practising the intonation. (5 mins)

5   **Now listen to the phrases again and practise the intonation.**

Tell the students that the planning department of Glaston City has to decide where to locate the proposed new city hospital. There are three possible locations.
Ask them to look at the plan of Glaston City Centre and at the three marked sites.   (20–30 mins)

6   **The planning department of Glaston City wants to build a new hospital but the authorities aren't sure which is the most suitable site.**
Three sites have been proposed. Look at the map of the city centre and take the following factors into consideration:

access

traffic

parking

noise

local residents' feelings

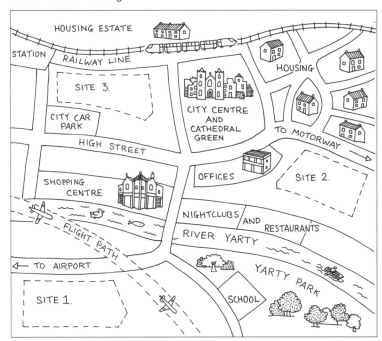

Divide the class into three groups. Each group represents a site.
In groups, they should talk about the pros of their site and the cons of the others. After 5 minutes, the groups present their arguments to the class. The class votes for the best site. (10–15 mins)

7   **In three groups representing the three sites, decide why you think your site is the best one.**
When you have worked out the reasons, tell the rest of the class why your site should be chosen.

4 Travel information

Tell the students to listen to the recording and to call out what the means of transport are. If there are different ideas, play the recording again to confirm. (5 mins)

1   Listen to the recording.
Which different kinds of transport can you recognise? 🔊 49

🔊 49
Sounds of:
   1
a motorbike
   2
an aeroplane
   3
a train
   4
a horse
   5
a car

Ask the students to match the two parts of the four dialogues. (5 mins)

2   Match the questions and the replies.

Questions	Replies
1 'I want to fly to Paris.'	4 'About an hour and a half.'
2 'Is there a train to Hamburg early on Monday morning?'	1 'And when do you want to go?'
3 'What are the times of the buses to the city centre, please?'	2 'The first one leaves at six am.'
4 'How long does the ferry take?'	3 'Every hour, on the hour.'

Tell the students to listen to the recording to check their answers. Then get them to practise the dialogues in pairs, paying attention to intonation patterns. (5–10 mins)

3   Listen to the recording to check your answers. 🔊 50

🔊 50
   1
Female voice 'I want to fly to Paris.'
Male voice 'And when do you want to go?'
   2
M 'Is there a train to Hamburg early on Monday morning?'
F   'The first one leaves at six am.'

3
M1 'What are the times of the buses to the city centre, please?'
M2 'Every hour, on the hour.'
4
F1 'How long does the ferry take?'
F2 'About an hour and a half.'

Put the students into small groups. Tell them to look at the pictures and to discuss what the two main advantages and drawbacks are of travelling using these methods. Walk around the class, monitoring and helping with vocabulary. (5–10 mins)

4   Look at the pictures. In groups, decide what the two main advantages and disadvantages are of travelling by each of these methods.

Advantages

_____

_____

_____

_____

_____

Disadvantages

_____

_____

_____

_____

_____

Get one student from each group to feedback briefly on one form of transport – all the students should have the opportunity to put forward an argument briefly and clearly.

Write up the words or phrases from activity 5 on the board. Explain any the students are not sure of. Ask them to discuss which ones they associate with forms of transport in their countries. You might need to do one together as a class to give them the scope of possibility. (5–10 mins)

5   **Which of the following words or phrases do you identify with which forms of transport? Why? Discuss in pairs.**

Dangerous

Stressful

Culture-shock

Environmentally friendly

Romantic

Freedom

Convenient

Anti-social

Move around the class monitoring, and have a brief feedback session: what was the most interesting thing their partner had to say?

Travel agency

Write 'train', 'boat', 'horse', 'bus', 'hire car', 'hire motorbike' on slips of paper (depending on class size), and put them into a bag. Put the class into the same number of groups as slips of paper. Each group draws out a type of transport. Tell them that each group works for a travel company selling holidays, using the method of transport on the slip. How can they make the transport a positive feature of their advertising campaign? Get them to choose a name for their company first, using the kind of transport they promote. They will also need to choose a group representative to give a minute-long presentation. Move around the class monitoring, suggesting ideas if necessary and helping with vocabulary. (10–15 mins)

6   **For this activity each group in the class represents a travel company. Choose the name of your company to suit the kind of transport it uses. Discuss how you can make the transport a positive feature of the kind of holiday your company sells.**
Then choose a group representative to 'sell' your holidays to the rest of the class.

Travel company name

Type of transport

Asking for travel information

Brainstorm things you might want to find out at a railway information office (eg, fares, times, class of tickets, refreshment facilities). Find out if anyone has ever had a problem travelling by train. What happened? (2–4 mins)

Tell the students they are at Paddington Station in London. Divide the class into two groups.
Group A students work in the information office.
Group B students are passengers wanting information about trains.
Students then roleplay and swap roles when they finish. Move around the class, monitoring each pair. (5–10 mins)

7 **Split up into two groups.**
Group A: You are receptionists at Paddington Station Information Centre. Using the information sheet below, help your customers.
Group B: You are rail customers. Using your role-cards get the different pieces of information you want – then Group A and Group B swap roles.

Group A

Paddington Railway Station Information Centre

Plymouth–Paddington (Monday–Friday)

DEP	ARR	Connections	Services	Single	Return
05·45	08·45		Trolley	£65·00	£110·00
06·45	09·45	Bristol for Bristol Airport	Buffet car	£65·00	£110·00
08·20	11·40		Buffet car	£35·50	£57·00
11·10	14·30	Bristol for Bristol Airport	Trolley	£35·50	£57·00
13·15	16·45			£35·50	£57·00
14·50	18·10			£35·50	£57·00
16·35	20·00		Buffet car	£35·50	£57·00
17·35	21·05		Buffet car	£35·50	£57·00
18·50	22·20		Buffet car	£35·50	£57·00
20·10	23·40		Trolley	£35·50	£57·00
00·10	05·40		Trolley	£30·00	£55·00 (seat)
				£45·00	£80·00 (sleeper)

Paddington–Plymouth (Monday–Friday)

DEP	ARR	Connections	Services	Single	Return
05·10	08·30		Trolley	£30·00	£55·00
07·30	10·40		Trolley	£30·00	£55·00
10·30	13·50	Plymouth Ferry	Buffet car	£30·00	£55·00
12·00	15·30		Buffet car	£35·50	£57·00
14·30	17·50			£35·50	£57·00
15·45	19·10			£35·50	£57·00
17·35	20·40	Plymouth Ferry	Buffet car	£65·00	£110·00
18·35	21·45		Buffet car	£65·00	£110·00
19·35	22·35		Buffet car	£65·00	£110·00
20·50	00·05			£30·00	£55·00
23·50	05·15		Trolley	£30·00	£55·00 (seat)
				£45·00	£80·00 (sleeper)

Group B

Role-card 1
You want to travel from Plymouth to Paddington on Tuesday morning. You're not in a hurry.
Find out about times, prices, and refreshment facilities .

Role-card 2
You need to get a connection to Bristol Airport on Friday afternoon. Check if there is a train.

Role-card 3
You want to travel to Paddington overnight. Ask about times and prices.

Role-card 4
You want to travel to Plymouth in the afternoon. You have to catch the Plymouth Ferry.

Role-card 5
You need to get to Paddington by midday on Monday.

Tell the students they are going to hear a recorded dialogue between a customer and a receptionist in a Coach Information Office. Ask them to underline the words which are stressed. Get them to compare answers with a partner. Then play the recording again and check their answers. Get them to practise the stress patterns in pairs, inserting alternative times, prices, etc. (5–10 mins)

---

8   **Listen to the recording and read the dialogue.**
    Underline the words that are stressed.
    Then compare your answers with a partner. 🔊 51

🔊 51

Receptionist 'Good morning, can I help you?'
Customer 'Yes. I want to book a coach to Bristol, please.'
R   'For today?'
C   'No, I'm travelling next Monday, that's the seventh of March.'
R   'Okay. Would you prefer to go in the morning or the afternoon?'
C   'Oh, the morning, please. As early as possible.'
R   'Right. Just let me see. Yes. There's one at six-thirty am and another one at seven.'
C   'Six-thirty! That is early! I'd prefer the seven o'clock one, please.'
R   'And will that be single or return?'
C   'Return, please. And how much does it cost?'
R   'That'll be twenty-five pounds.'

---

9   **Listen again to check and then practise the dialogue with your partner, replacing the days, times and prices with different information.**

5 Ranking – what comes first?

The best days of your life?

Engage the students' interest in the subject of school days by asking them to listen to the dialogues about different aspects of school life and then discussing what each dialogue is about. (5 mins)

1 **Listen to the recordings about school life.** 🔊 52

🔊 52

1

Male voice **'You can remember Mr Williams, can't you?'**
Female voice 'Of course, I can. He was really nice.'
M **'Nice! I thought he was terrible.'**
F 'Really? In what way?'
M **'He was so boring. And he always took ages to get to the point in his lessons.'**
F 'But he was very patient too … and kind.'
M **'Not to me, he wasn't!'**

2

F 'How much did you have to do last night?'
M **'About three hours. I had to finish my chemistry project and do an essay. How about you?'**
F 'I just had some revision for today's geography test. I hope I've done enough!'

3

F 'Look at this photo. That's me at High School.'
M **'What on earth are you wearing?'**
F 'A green blazer, tie, white shirt and straw hat.'
M **'Did you have to wear that?'**
F 'Yes, of course. Didn't you?'
M **'No – we were free to wear what we liked.'**

Ask the students to think about their first year at school. Tell them to make notes of some good and bad memories they have from that time. Ask them to compare their different experiences with a partner. How different are their partner's memories? You can have a brief feedback session of the best and worst memories. (5–10 mins)

2 **Can you remember your first year at school? Make notes of some good and bad memories you have from that time. Tell your partner. How different are your partner's memories?**

Ask the students to think of a teacher they liked. Brainstorm the things they remember about the person. You can put these up on the board, eg, 'was funny', 'very interested in his subject', 'didn't give us much homework.' (5 mins)

3 **Think of a teacher you liked. Make notes of things you remember about him or her. Compare your notes with your partner. Are there any similarities?**

Now ask them to think of a teacher they disliked. Tell them to write down a list of reasons (just as they did in the brainstorming session). Ask them to try to put these reasons in order of importance. Tell them to compare their lists with a partner and to find the differences. (5–10 mins)

4   **Have you ever had a teacher you disliked? Try to make a list in order of importance of the reasons for your dislike. Compare your lists with your partner. What are the differences?**

Tell the students to look at the reasons for going to school. Ask them which they think are the most important and the least important? Then ask them to try to fit the rest of the reasons in order. For each choice, they should think about why. Get them to write the numbers 1 (most important) to 10 (least important) next to their choices. (5 mins)

5   **Look at the reasons below for going to school.
Which do you think are the most important and the least important?
Put the reasons in order of importance from 1 (most important)
to 10 (least important). For each choice, think about why.**

Why do you go to school?	1 to 10	Why?
To learn right from wrong		
To prepare for a job by learning specific skills		
To make friends		
To learn how to think for yourself		
To learn how to interact with different sorts of people		
To broaden general knowledge		
To pass exams		
To allow parents to go out to work		
To learn how to use books and technology		
To have a good time		

Put the students into small groups to discuss their choices and to try to persuade the others to change their minds. Ask them to try to reach a general agreement in their groups. Get them briefly to feedback to the rest of the class on those things they can't agree on and why. Move around the groups, making sure all the students contribute to the discussion. (15 mins)

6   **In groups, discuss your choices and try to persuade the others to change their minds. Can you reach a general agreement in your groups? Briefly feed back to the rest of the class on those things you cannot agree about and why.**

Give the students additional ranking practice with activities 7 to 14. Monitor, and make sure that the students understand and use the language correctly. Note any language models that will need further study at the end of the activities. (Allow 3–5 mins for the activities on a teacher's qualities and shopping, and 5–10 mins for the activities on eating out.)

7   **Which qualities do you think make a good teacher?**
Put the following in order of importance from 1 (most important) to 10 (least important) and make some notes about why.

Qualities	1 to 10	Why?
knowledge of subject		
love of subject		
experience		
smart clothes		
good sense of humour		
ability to communicate		
attractiveness		
punctuality and efficiency		
fairness to all students		
strong discipline		

8   **Compare your list with a partner. If you disagree, find out why.**

Shopping for clothes

9 **When you are shopping for clothes, which of the following questions are most important to you? Put them in order of importance from 1 (most important) to 10 (least important). Make some notes about why and compare your lists with your partner.**

Questions	1 to 10	Why?
How fashionable is it?		
Does it suit me?		
How much is it?		
What is it made of?		
How well-made is it?		
Which company made it?		
Will it wash well?		
Do I have shoes that suit the outfit?		
Can I wear it for different occasions?		
Will it last a long time?		

Eating out

10 **You and your partner are entering the 'Best menu' competition. You must think of a menu of three courses for two people which is delicious, is relatively cheap and healthy, and can be cooked in one evening. Talk about these things and then agree on your menu.**

Menu

Starter

Main course

Dessert

11 **Now look at everyone's menus. Which one do you like best and want to vote for? You can't vote for your own!**

12 You are responsible for arranging an evening out in a restaurant for your class. Look at the different types of restaurant. Write notes about what you like or dislike about each of these. Then rank them 1 (best) to 10 (worst) as the most suitable food to eat on the class night out.

Restaurant	Like	Dislike	1 to 10
Italian			
Indian			
Chinese			
Vegetarian			
Japanese			
French			
Thai			
Greek			
Fast food			
Local speciality			

13 Put the following aspects of eating in a restaurant in order of importance to you.

Qualities	1 to 10	Why?
friendly waiters		
delicious food		
wide choice of food		
cleanliness		
lighting		
décor		
smoking and non-smoking areas		
background music		
quick service		
good value for money		

14 Explain your choices to your partner and find out how far you agree.

6 Making hotel bookings

Write up 'Can you help me? I'd like to book...' on the board.
Brainstorm things people might want to book. (2 mins)

Tell the students to listen to the recording. What do they think these
people are booking? (5–10 mins)

Then play the recording again to check their answers and answer
any structural or vocabulary queries they have.

1 **Listen to the recording and write down what the people are booking.**
   🔊 53

   1 smoking table in a restaurant for six people at 7.30 pm

   2 4 tickets for *The Wind in the Willows* matinee at the theatre

   3 a campsite, next to the river, for the weekend

   4 a first-class ticket to Guildford

🔊 53
   1
Female voice 'I'd like to book a table for tonight, please.'
Male voice 'Certainly, madam. For how many?'
F **'For six, please.'**
M 'And at what time?'
F **'Around seven-thirty?'**
M 'A table for six people at seven-thirty. No problem. Do you want smoking
   or non-smoking?'
F **'Smoking, please.'**
M 'That's fine. We look forward to seeing you tonight.'
   2
M **'I want to book four tickets for *The Wind in the Willows*, for Saturday
   the 8th of March, please.'**
F 'The matinée or the evening performance?'
M **'The matinée, please.'**
F 'Stalls or circle?'
M **'The front stalls, please. In the middle, if possible.'**
F 'Just let me have a look. Yes, we've got D 16 to 19.'
M **'That'd be fine. How much are the tickets?'**
F 'Adults or children?'
M **'Two adults and two children.'**
F 'Adults are sixteen pounds and children seven pounds.'
M **'That's fine. Can I pay by card?'**
F 'Yes, of course.'

3

F **'I want to book a site for the weekend of the 20th of this month, please.'**

M 'For a tent or a caravan?'

F **'A tent.'**

M 'And for how many people?'

F **'Just two of us. We've been before and we'd like the same place, if possible, in the far field next to the river.'**

M 'Yes. That should be possible. Now let me take your details…'

4

M **'Can I help you, please?'**

F 'Yes, I want to book a ticket from Guildford to Waterloo, tomorrow.'

M **'Round about what time?'**

F 'Round about one pm if possible.'

M **'Just a minute and I'll take a look … yes, okay, there's one leaving Guildford at one-fifteen and it arrives at Waterloo station at two-twenty.'**

F 'Yes, that's ideal.'

M **'Is that first or standard class?'**

F 'First, please.'

M **'That'll be thirteen pounds eighty, please.'**

Ask the students to brainstorm some names of hotels they have stayed in. Ask them which hotels they liked best and which least. Ask why.

Then ask them to look at the pictures. Which of these things are important to them when they are booking a hotel? Are there any things which aren't on the list which are important (eg, cost, friendly staff, food)? (5 mins)

2 **What's important to you when you choose a hotel?**
Look at these hotel facilities:

Put the following facilities in order of importance from 1 (most important) to 7 (least important).
Talk to your partner about each facility and see if you agree or disagree on your choices.

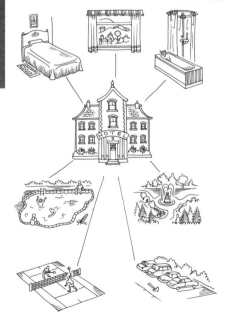

Facilities	1 to 7
bed	
view from window	
bath/shower	
car park	
tennis court	
landscaped garden	
swimming pool	

Booking a holiday

Tell the students that when you are booking something, you need to give clear and precise information and to ask direct and clear questions. Tell them to listen to the recording. Ask them to decide how clear (or unclear) the customers are in each situation. Ask them why this is. Then play the recording again to check their answers. (5–10 mins)

**3 Listen to two people booking a hotel room.
Do they know what they want and ask for it clearly?
Make some notes below.** ▱ 54

What they want	Are they clear?

▱ 54

1

Female voice 'Good morning, Garrack Hotel. How can I help you?'
Male voice 'Er … I want a room, please.'
F 'Certainly, sir. When for?'
M 'For Saturday and Sunday. And how much is it?'
F 'Well, sir, our prices vary depending on the season. Is it for this Saturday and Sunday?'
M 'No, no, in May. The first weekend.'
F 'Right, so May the second and third. And do you want a single or double room?'
M 'For my wife and myself. And we want a bathroom with the room.'
F 'Right. So a double room, en-suite. Is it just bed-and-breakfast or do you want half- or full-board?'
M 'How much is it?'
F 'Well, sir, let me take you through the price list…'

2

F 'Good afternoon, Garrack Hotel. How can I help you?'
M 'I'd like to book a single en-suite room, please, for the third of July only.'
F 'Certainly, sir. Is that bed-and-breakfast only?'
M 'That's right. And I'd prefer non-smoking, please.'
F 'Yes. That's no problem.'
M 'How much will that be?'
F 'It's forty pounds per night.'
M 'That's fine. And do you have a guest car park?'
F 'Yes, we do.'
M 'Right. Can I give you my details…?'

Before the class, cut out a variety of holiday advertisements from current travel brochures. Vary the types of holiday and make sure that travel times, costs, accommodation, etc, are included.

Put the class in pairs. Tell the students they are going to roleplay booking a two-week holiday. They take turns to be the customer. The travel agency information which you have prepared is the same for both turns: it is the customer's needs that are different. While they are roleplaying, monitor for fluency and communication. (15–30 mins)

4   **Working with a partner, roleplay the following situation:**
Student A: You want to book a two-week holiday for you and a friend. You ring the Take a Break travel agency. You need to be clear about the following:

destination

kind of holiday (sun/sea, sporty, luxury etc)

dates and times (departure and return)

departure airport (flight number)

kind of accommodation

costs

Student B: You work in the bookings office of the Take a Break travel agency. Using information from holiday brochures provided by your teacher, help your customer book a suitable holiday. The brochures should contain information about:

resort name

activities available

dates and times

flight numbers

hotel/facilities

costs

Again put the class in pairs. Tell the students they are going to roleplay booking a room at the Carnegie Hotel. (15–20 mins)

5   Now roleplay a different situation.
Student A: You want to book some rooms for you and your family at the Carnegie Hotel. You need to give information about the following:

dates – arrival / departure

number and type of rooms required

special requirements (child's cot in room, etc)

credit card number

name and contact number

You also want to find out about :

Rooms – all with bathroom, TV, tea- and coffee-making facilities?

Restaurant – kind of food?

Swimming pool and fitness room?

Cost?

Student B: You are the receptionist at the Carnegie Hotel. Look at the information opposite. Help your customer to book the accommodation required. You also want to find out about the following:

Do they want B&B (bed-and-breakfast), half board (breakfast and dinner) or full board (breakfast, lunch and dinner)?

Which dates?

How many rooms?

Car parking required?

Any special requests?

Write 'I'd've loved to've gone, but I didn't have time' on the board. Elicit the full form: 'I would have loved to have gone, but I did not have time'. Write it up. Now get half the class to say the first, and the other half the second. Tell them that spoken English uses a lot of contracted forms.

Tell the students they're going to listen for contracted forms in the following dialogues. Ask them to write down the ones they notice. Play the recording. Then play the dialogues a second time to confirm their answers. If you think it's useful, the students can listen and practise them as a whole class. (5 mins)

THE CARNEGIE HOTEL

Situated on the edge of Dartmoor, in grounds of five acres, this is an ideal hotel from which to explore the surrounding country-side. Carnegie Hotel is 15km from the lovely town of Polton and only two km from the M16 motorway. All rooms have bath/shower, satellite TV and tea- and coffee-making facilities.
There are two restaurants

The Lime Tree

(7.30am–11.30pm)

An all-day family café. Serving a range of hot and cold snacks, desserts, sandwiches and drinks.

∙∙∙

The Green Lion Restaurant

(12.00 noon–2.30pm and 7.30–11.30pm)

A four-star restaurant specialising in traditional dishes made with fresh, local ingredients.
Breakfast served in the Green Lion Restaurant from 7.00–10.00am

∙∙∙

Two bars – one with games room (pool, snooker, billiards)
Indoor heated swimming pool with sauna and solarium
Mini-golf course
Ample car parking facilities
Local tours booked from the hotel

∙∙∙

PRICES

Double room	
(per person – based on two people sharing)	
B&B	£65
B&B and evening meal	£85
Full board	£97
Single room (per person)	
B&B	£75
B&B and evening meal	£90
Full board	£105

6   **Listen for the contracted forms on the recording and note them down. Then listen again and check your answers.** 📼 55

📼 55

1

F   **'Did you have good seats for the concert?'**

M   'Well, I'd have preferred to have been a bit closer to the stage.'

2

M   **'There'll be fireworks at the party, you know.'**

F   'Really? It'll be a disaster if John's in charge. You know what he's like.'

3

F   **'Aaaagh! This water's freezing. You should've warned me!'**

M   'Don't worry. You'll get used to it.'

4

M   **'You've made this garden look beautiful, you know.'**

F   'Well, I couldn't have done it without Mark's help.'

7 Filling in forms

What do I put here?

Tell the students to listen to the recording. Ask them to think about where the people are and what are they doing. (5–10 mins)

**1 Listen to the recording.
Where are the people and what are they doing?** 🔊 56

🔊 56

1

M **'So, madam, which flight did you say you were on?'**

F 'Flight SR20 from Seoul. Arriving at fourteen-twenty.'

M **'And what exactly has gone missing?'**

F 'My suitcase.'

M **'Your full name, please.'**

F 'Josephine Scuffil – that's SCU double F IL. Miss.'

M **'And a description of the suitcase, please?'**

F 'It's a large, black leather suitcase, on wheels. About one and a half metres by a metre.

M **'Any distinguishing features?'**

F 'Yes. It's got a large, red stripe across the front and gold coloured handles…'

2

F **'And it's a full student ticket you want, is it?'**

M 'That's right. Travelling daily from Crediton to Exeter. But not weekends.'

F **'So, let's have your details. Name?'**

M 'Ian Urry.'

F **'Sorry?'**

M 'U double R Y. Urry.'

F **'And your date of birth?'**

M '21 – 7 – 86.'

F **'Are you a full- or part-time student?'**

M 'Full-time.'

F **'Where is your place of study?'**

M 'Exeter College.'

F **'And at what times will you be mainly travelling?'**

M 'Between 8 and 9 in the morning and 4 and 6 in the evening.'

F **'Okay. Now, if you'd just like to sign here…'**

3

M 'How long do you intend to be visiting the Gambia?'

F **'For about one month.'**

M 'And what is your reason for travel?'

F **'Business.'**

M 'So. Your surname please?'

F **'Chang.'**

M 'And your first names?'

F **'Amy.'**

M 'Nationality?'

F **'British.'**

M 'Do you have your passport number?'

F **'Yes, it's CL 431700.'**

M 'Date of travel?'

F **'The seventh of September…'**

Get the students to write down all the different forms they've had to complete in the last five years. Give them a 1–2 minute time-limit. Get them to compare their list with their partner. Then, as a class, check out any unusual ones.

---

2 **When do you have to fill in forms? Write down all the different types of form you've filled in during the last five years.**
You've got 2 minutes! Compare your list with your partner.

Get the students to match the questions on the left with the answers on the right. Then check as a class, clearing up any problems. (5–10 mins)

3 **Match the questions on the left and the answers on the right.**

Questions	Answers
1 First name/Forename/Given name	10 IBC Computers (1993–2003)
2 Surname	5 British
3 Country of birth	4 Mr
4 Title	8 Single
5 Nationality	9 Computer analyst
6 DOB/date of birth	1 Andrew
7 Telephone/fax number	6 16/02/1971
8 Marital status	12 £26,500
9 Occupation	7 020 4312 7698
10 Relevant experience	3 Scotland
11 Email address	2 Campbell
12 Present salary	11 ajcam@aol.com.uk

Job applications

Tell the students they are going to roleplay filling in a job application form at a recruitment agency (agents and clients). Have the students sitting opposite each other so they don't see each other's information. At the end of each interaction, the students swap roles, using a different role-card. The agents can write down the information. The agents can advise on the suitable jobs on offer (page 133).

While the students are activating the language, monitor and listen closely for question-forming errors and correct these.

4 **Work with a partner and act out the roleplay.**

Student A: You work for a recruitment agency (a company that matches potential employees and job vacancies).
You need to fill in the application form with the applicant's details.
Ask Student B for the relevant information. Try to match him or her with an appropriate job from the list given on page 96.

Student B: You are looking for a job. Give Student A the details he or she needs to fill in your application form.

Application Form
_____

Surname
_____

Given name
_____

Address
_____

_____

Phone (day/evening)
_____

Fax
_____

Email
_____

DOB
_____

Qualifications
_____

Work experience
_____

Previous or present job
_____

Reason for leaving
_____

Previous/present salary
_____

Job wanted
_____

Strengths, skills, abilities
_____

Job vacancies

5 **Work with a partner and act out the roleplay.**

Student A: You work for a recruitment agency. Help Student B find the right job to apply for, and ask him or her for the information you need.

Student B: You are looking for a job. You contact the recruitment agency. Ask about the jobs on offer and decide which one you want to apply for.

The recruitment agency will need to know:

personal details
_____

details of your CV (a curriculum vitae lists your education and work record to date)
_____

the kind of job you want
_____

Job vacancies

Driver
Must have clean driving licence. Will be driving transit van and delivering electrical supplies.
8am–5pm. £11,000 per annum

Administrator
To work in city office. Duties include answering telephone, data input onto computer, checking invoices.
15–25 hours per week. £6.00 per hour

Receptionist
For city centre health clinic. Communication and client skills required. Main duties will be making appointments and dealing with queries. Must have maths and English qualifications.
30 hours per week. £12,000 per annum

Care assistant
Must be aged over 18. Previous experience preferred, but not essential as training will be given. You will be caring for elderly people, including washing, dressing and feeding.
20 hours per week – times to be arranged. £5.50 per hour

Pizza chef
To work in a busy pizza restaurant, cooking pizzas to order, preparing toppings, salads and vegetables. Must be able to work under pressure as part of a friendly team.
40 hour week, shifts 10am–5pm or 5pm–midnight.
£5.90 per hour plus monthly bonus.

Telesales account manager
Good interpersonal and communication skills needed. Working in a busy call centre undertaking outgoing telephone calls.
Commission based on sales. £11,000 basic plus commission.

Swimming pool lifeguard
To work in popular sport centre. Duties include lifeguarding, cleaning and maintenance work.
Must hold lifeguarding qualification.
35 hours per week. £5.60 per hour

Customer adviser
Sales or retail experience preferred to work in a high street bank.
Confident telephone manner required for selling and advising on financial matters.
25 hours per week. £8.50 per hour.

Ask the students to look at the form for joining a language school. Tell them to listen to the recording and to complete the information on the form. Then get them to listen again, to check their answers and to be aware of the question formation. (5–10 mins)

6 **Look at the form for joining the International Language School. Listen to the recording and complete the information on the form.** 📼 57

International Language School

Full name Pablo Calderon

Title Mr

DOB 3/8/71

Country of birth Venezuela

First language Spanish

English study (number of years) 9 years

Occupation communications engineer

Level of English intermediate

Language areas you are good at speaking

Language areas you need to improve listening

Full- or part-time course full-time

Accommodation: host family/hotel/private host family

Date you wish to start 10 July

Length of course required 8 weeks

Contact number and address 0406 79027

📼 57

Male voice 'I'd like to take a course at your school. I've seen the brochure and I'm interested.'
Female voice 'Good. Then let me take all your details. First … what is your full name?'
M 'It's Pablo Calderon. Mr Pablo Calderon.'
F 'Thank you. And when were you born?'
M '3 – 8 – 71.'
F 'And where were you born?'
M 'In Venezuela.'
F 'And what is your first language?'
M 'Spanish.'
F 'So, Pablo, how long have you been learning English?'
M 'Hm, let me think, it's about nine years.'
F 'And are you a full-time student at the moment?'
M 'No. I'm a communications engineer. My company are paying for me to take an English course.'
F 'What would you say your level of English is?'
M 'Well, I should say I'm at an intermediate level.'

F 'Good. And what skills in English are you good at?'

M 'Well, my speaking's quite good, but I need to improve my listening. I find it very difficult to understand what people are saying.'

F 'Are you looking for a full- or part-time course?'

M 'Full-time, please. I need it!'

F 'What kind of accommodation would you prefer?'

M 'I'd definitely prefer living with a host family. That way I can improve my listening in the evenings.'

F 'And when do you want to start?'

M 'On the tenth of July.'

F 'And how long for?'

M 'Eight weeks.'

F 'That's fine, Pablo. We look forward to having you in the school. Now what's your phone number?'

M 'It's 040679027.'

F 'Thank you.'

7 Listen to the recording again, check your answers and also listen carefully to how the questions are formed.

Ask the students to practise asking and answering the questions using their own information. (5–10 mins)

8 Practise asking and answering the questions with your own information.

8 Questionnaires

Things I've always wanted to know but have never liked to ask!

Ask the students to listen to the different people on the recording and to say what they all have in common. (They are all asking people to fill in questionnaires.) (5–10 mins)

1 **Listen to the recording. What do all the people have in common?** 📼 58

📼 58

1

Female voice 1 **'I wonder if I could just have a few minutes of your time…?'**

2

Male voice 1 'Could I ask you to answer a few questions for me, please…?'

3

Female voice 2 **'I'm ringing on behalf of Launa Windows to ask you if you…?'**

4

Male voice 2 'Would you mind taking the time to look at this leaflet and to answer…?'

5

Female voice 3 **'I work for Consumer Services and we're trying to find out what…?'**

Brainstorm all the different kinds of questionnaire the students have ever answered. Write them on the board. Ask if they like/dislike doing them. Are they an invasion of privacy? What's the point of them? Do the students always answer truthfully?

Tell the students that they are going to devise their own questionnaires on a topic which is of genuine interest to them. (20–30 mins)

2 **Imagine you are doing a survey on a topic for a magazine (eg, sport, health, TV, films, food, perfect partner, studying English, art, family, feelings).**
Choose a topic you are interested in and that you would like to ask the rest of your class about. Write down the 10 to 20 questions that would be most useful in helping you to research your topic.
First, look at the different questionnaire types:

How often do you go to the gym? (Choose A, B, C or D)
A Never
B Once a month
C Once a week
D More than once a week

Do you like fast food?	Yes	No

What's your all-time favourite film?

At a job interview are you terrified?	excited?	slightly nervous?	confident?

Now tell the students to devise their own questionnaires. Where necessary, help them to write their questions in a way that suits the questionnaire type they have chosen.

Tell them to take their questionnaires around the class, asking as many students as they can in the given time-limit. (5 mins)

3 Move around the class asking other students the questions and filling in the information.

At the end of this session, get the students to examine their results. Does their questionnaire show, for example, that 90% of the class likes fast food? Ask students to report back to the rest of the class with the most surprising thing they have each learnt. (5–10 mins)

4 At the end of the session report back to the class on the most surprising thing you have learnt.

Tell the students to listen to the recording. Ask them to decide who the market researchers work for. Let them discuss their ideas with a partner. Check their answers. (5–10 mins)

5 Listen to the recording.
Who do you think these market researchers work for?
Discuss your answers with your partner. 📼 59

📼 59
1
Female voice 1 '**I wonder if you'd mind answering some questions for me, please? I work on behalf of ...... and we are asking people what features they look for when they are buying a new model – speed, safety, cost, comfort, look and colour, and so on...'**
2
Male voice 1 'Would you be so kind as to give me a few minutes of your time? I work for ...... and I want to ask some questions about your last holiday. Have you taken a holiday in the last year?
3
Female voice 2 '**Oh, hello. I'm ringing on behalf of ...... It's a new company and we guarantee our calls, both national and international, are half the cost of other companies. We don't believe in peak-time charges and calls to family members are free...'**
4
Male voice 2 'Could I ask you to answer a few questions for me, please? I belong to ...... and we are looking for more volunteers to campaign against all kinds of hunting for pleasure. What do you feel about ......?'

Then play the recording again. This time confirm the answers (car company, travel company, phone company, anti-hunting organisation). Then get the students to practise the intonation of the introductory phrases.

6 Now listen to the recording again to check your answers.

Test practice

The organisation of the test practice is a matter for your judgement in the particular teaching situation you are in. With larger classes, it can be difficult to use the practice test as an activity in class time. You can ask the students to practise in pairs, with one adopting the role of interlocutor, but if it is possible to conduct the practice exercise (and at some stage a full practice test) yourself or have a fellow teacher do so, it will be valuable test preparation.

(This type of task would normally take only a few minutes in the test itself and one of the test skills to cultivate is a fluent exchange of information/comment in a short time.)

Test practice – Achiever

**The following task is similar to the one you will carry out with the
interlocutor in Part 3 of the Spoken ESOL test at Achiever level.
The interlocutor will start by saying:**

'… in this part of the test we are going to ask and answer questions to make
some decisions.

'You and I have decided to open a new restaurant in this town. Let's talk about
the things in the pictures. Then let's decide what kind of restaurant we want to
open and who would use it.'

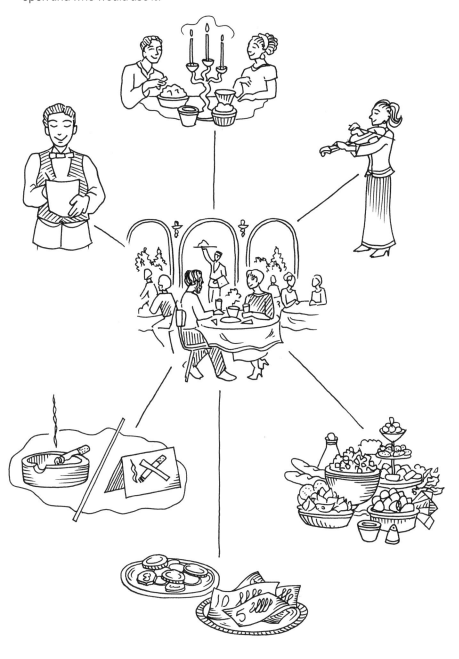

Test practice – Communicator

**The following task is similar to the one you will carry out with the interlocutor in Part 3 of the Spoken ESOL test at Communicator level.
The interlocutor will start by saying:**

'... in this part of the test we're going to ask and answer questions to exchange information and make some plans.'

'Here is your diary for next week and some details about what's on at the cinema. My diary and cinema details are different. Let's decide where to go and when.'

Interlocutor's Sheet

Monday	**Friday**
Working late	

Tuesday	**Saturday**
Tennis Club 7–9pm	Day trip to Brighton

Wednesday	**Sunday**

Thursday	
Tom & Laura to dinner	

The Film Centre

Screen 1	Scream 3	(16.15, 20.45)
Screen 2	Desert Sun	(18.30, 21.30)
Screen 3	Close Friends	(19.15, 22.00)

Note: What about eating?

Candidate's Sheet

Monday	**Friday**

Tuesday	**Saturday**
Meeting with Bill 5–7pm	

Wednesday	**Sunday**
Swimming 6.30pm	Gill and Pete coming 8pm

Thursday	

Picture House

Screen 1	Animal Fun	(16.00)
Screen 2	Space Episode	(19.15)
Screen 3	Out of the Blue	(21.00)

Note: Go in my car?

Introduction to Part 4

In Part 4 of this book, students build the skills necessary to speak about a single topic for an extended period. In Part 4 of the Spoken ESOL test, they will be asked to demonstrate this skill by speaking on a topic that the interlocutor will give them. The topics will never require specialist knowledge and candidates will be examined on the communicative use of English, never on opinions expressed. Candidates will have a short time to think and will be given pencil and paper to make some notes if they want. Though short, time spent preparing is very valuable; candidates who have organised their thoughts invariably perform more competently and confidently than those who have not. The skill of managing and maintaining continuous speech requires a lot of practice and at Achiever and Communicator levels students are still at the stage of developing range and fluency in order to produce an extended turn. Candidates often underestimate the amount that can be covered in even two or three minutes. The activities in this part of the book give students the chance to gradually acquire these skills.

You will want to help students think about the features that make a presentation effective. Timing their presentations will give them a realistic idea of the test. The recordings that accompany the units give examples of people speaking naturally at reasonable length and provide a model of the type of production of language that will help candidates succeed in the test.

After the talk has finished, the interlocutor will ask some follow-up questions. Students need to practise listening carefully in order to be able to give an appropriate response. As the candidate is in control of his or her presentation, a reasonable degree of lexical and grammatical accuracy will be expected at the Achiever and Communicator levels. You will probably find yourself monitoring closely during pair/group activities and, without breaking the flow of language, correcting mistakes and encouraging students to recognise, anticipate and eliminate errors as far as possible without losing fluency.

4

Part 4 Presenting a topic

There are times when you will want to talk in some detail about a topic. You may be asked to give a report at work or at college; you may want to tell your friends about your views on keeping fit or an important new law you read about in the newspaper. The units that follow will help you build your skills in speaking for a few minutes on a single topic.

In Part 4 of the Spoken ESOL test you will be given a topic on which to speak. You'll have a short time to prepare. The units that follow will give you practice in talking about the kinds of things you might be asked on the exam: entertainment you enjoy, the pros and cons of tourism, the advantages and disadvantages of being rich and famous, your favourite way to spend a weekend, and so on. Take turns speaking and listening to other speakers – both will help you to develop your range and fluency.

Tips from the examiners

The more you practise speaking for an extended period, the more confident and fluent you will become. Be sure you give several short presentations before the exam. You might want to time your talks. You will probably be surprised at how much you can cover in just a few minutes if you plan in advance. When you finish your talk, the interlocutor will ask you a few questions. Listen carefully so that you respond directly to what is being asked.

1 That's entertainment!

Engage the students' interest in the topic by announcing that the class has won a prize – a free visit to an evening of entertainment. Brainstorm! Ask for ideas for types of entertainment and put suitable suggestions on the board.

Explain that the class will be divided into pairs/groups and that each pair/group will argue the case for one type of entertainment. Organise the pairs/groups as best fits your teaching situation (allow students to form pairs/groups; you choose the pairs/groups; draw names from a hat, etc).

Instruct the pairs/groups to argue for one of the types of entertainment on the list. It usually works best if the teacher draws lots to decide which pair/group argues for which item – the focus is on the students' speaking skills of explaining, expanding and persuading, and not on any 'best' option. (2–3 mins)

Instruct the pairs/groups to produce as many arguments as they can think of for their type of entertainment. Monitor, and prompt if necessary – stress that the students don't really need to agree with their own arguments; the objective is to try to persuade others. Supply language of explanation, persuasion wherever helpful: 'What I mean is…' 'Everyone agrees that…' etc.

Organise the class for the presentation of arguments. Explain that each pair/group will have 2 minutes to present their case without interruption. At the end of the 2 minutes, the other groups (in a free-for-all debate) can put questions or raise counter-arguments for 1 minute. (10–15 mins)

Set up an order for pairs/groups to present their case – the simplest way is probably to draw lots.

1 **Your class has won a prize – a free visit to enjoy an evening of entertainment of your choice.**
   You are going to argue for one type of entertainment.
   Work with your partner to prepare as many arguments as you can.
   Give details of the event you are arguing for.

Type of entertainment	Event details
cinema	
sports event	
classical music concert	
circus	
musical	
ballet	
other	

The students present their case. Prompt if any of the students dries up and ensure that at this stage the other students in the class listen without interrupting.

Signal when time is up and allow other pairs/groups to put questions or counter-arguments. Act as question-master and keep the open-ended debate flowing with maximum opportunity for students to fire questions and to respond.

When all pairs/groups have presented their arguments and taken questions the class decides whose argument was most persuasive. (3 mins per group)

2 **You have 2 minutes to argue your case and then the other pairs or groups can ask questions for you to answer. Finally, decide who wins!**

Engage the students' interest in the decision by recapitulating the arguments put for or against each case. (5 mins)

Instruct the students to discuss in pairs/groups the arguments they have heard. Each group votes for the best three arguments (excluding their own!) and awards 3 points for the best, 2 for the next best and 1 for the third. Each group writes down their vote and hands it to the teacher. Read out the results of the voting, putting the scores on the board or overhead projector. (5 mins)

Now decide who wins! Round up the debate and voting by drawing the students' attention to language of persuasion successfully used and adding other exponents as you think appropriate. (5 mins)

Live or on TV?

Engage the students' interest in the topic by asking what events they have watched live or on TV. Brainstorm! Ask the students to contribute types of event and put these on the board (along with types of entertainment already discussed, you can add festivals, state occasions, natural events such as an eclipse, etc). **(5 mins)**

3   **Is it better to watch events (sports, music concerts, special occasions and so on) live or on TV?**
    This is a question that people often debate. What arguments would you give for and against the statement below?
    Here are one or two examples – discuss them with your partner and add any more you can think of.

Statement	For	Against
'It is better to watch events live than to watch them on TV.'	You're part of the atmosphere.'	'It can be boring.'
	'It's exciting.'	'It's expensive.'

Organise students into groups and instruct them to discuss the pros and cons of watching events live against watching them on TV. Monitor, and prompt if students lack ideas. **(5–10 mins)**

Elicit responses from the students and put some of these on the board. Focus on the language of explanation and justification, using the students' contributions and adding others as you think appropriate. **(10 mins)**

Engage the students' interest in listening to the recording by explaining that they are going to hear two people arguing for or against the statement, 'It is better to watch events live than to watch them on TV.' **(2 mins)**

Instruct the students to listen to the tape and, in groups, decide which speaker 'wins' the debate and why. **(5 mins)**

4   **Listen to two people arguing for or against the statement and decide who wins and why.** 🔘 60

📟 60

1

Male voice 'It's got to be live! It doesn't matter whether it's sport, music, drama ... whatever it is, it's better if you're actually there; part of it. I know that sometimes it can be uncomfortable – crowded, too hot or too cold, but that doesn't bother me at all; the atmosphere makes up for it. If you go to a football match, for example, you have all the excitement of the game. If you're at a music concert, you hear a unique performance every single time. Never mind the cost, the discomfort or anything else – live is life!'

2

Female voice 'For me, there's no argument. Watching something on TV has all the advantages. You can see everything – from all angles – and of course it's much more comfortable. If I'm at home watching something on TV, I can make myself a cup of coffee, sit on the sofa and relax. If you go to see a play or listen to a concert live, you have to pay – tickets these days cost a fortune! If you stay at home and watch TV, you don't have to waste time and money travelling either.'

Elicit the students' comments about which speaker uses the most persuasive argument and focus on the ways in which the effective organisation and production of language made the presentation successful. (5–10mins)

Instruct the students to listen to the recording again to see if any of their contributions were the same as those made by the speakers. (5 mins)

Elicit feedback from the students and discuss which arguments were the same as theirs and which were different. Focus on the language used by the speakers and draw the students' attention to the use of stress and intonation patterns to emphasise various points: 'It's much better', 'There's nothing better', etc. (5–10mins)

2 The trip of a lifetime!

Engage the students' interest by announcing that the class has the chance to take the trip of a lifetime. Brainstorm! Ask the students to suggest what would make something 'the trip of a lifetime' and put some of the contributions on the board. (2–3 mins)

1   Your class has the chance to take the trip of a lifetime. All expenses are paid. All you have to do is to decide which trip to choose.
You are going to argue for one of the dream trips listed below.
Work with a partner to prepare as many arguments as you can for your type of trip. Give some details about what you think the trip will include.

Option	Details
One-day return flights to any city of your choice	
A train journey across a continent	
One-week cruise on a luxury ocean liner	
A week of culture in any country of your choice	
An expedition to the Antarctic	
A hot-air balloon flight over a wildlife reserve	
A month camping in the Australian Outback	
A boat trip up one of the world's great rivers	

Refer the students to the trips on the list and explain any vocabulary which might be unfamiliar: cruise, expedition, etc. (5 mins)

Organise the students into groups and instruct them to prepare the case for their dream trip. Make sure each group has a sufficiently different type of trip to argue for (it is often best to draw lots to see which group gets which category or has the opportunity to choose their category first). Monitor while the students are preparing their arguments, and prompt where necessary. (10 mins)

Choose the order in which the groups make their presentations – again, it might be simplest to draw lots. Make sure that each group has a full 2 minutes without interruption, prompting any group that seems likely to dry up. At the end of each presentation, encourage the other students to put questions and raise objections. If you need to contribute to give the students the chance to expand on their arguments, you might like to put forward negative aspects of each case. (3 mins per group)

2   **Now you have 2 minutes to argue your case and then the other pairs or groups can ask questions for you to answer.**

Engage the students' interest in the next activity by explaining that they are going to vote for the winners – the group which put forward the most persuasive arguments for the trip of a lifetime. Recapitulate some of the main points made by each group, giving a corrected version of the actual language used where necessary. (2–3 mins)

Instruct the students in their groups to discuss the arguments they have heard. Monitor, and remind the students to say which arguments persuaded them. Ask the students to write their votes on a secret ballot paper and hand them to you. It often produces lively discussion if you ask groups to give 3 points to the best argument, 2 points to the second best and 1 point to the third best. (5–10mins)

3   **Discuss with your partner the arguments you heard for the different trips. Which were the best arguments? Vote for the best three. (Sorry, you can't vote for your own team!)**

Read out the votes and give the results. (3–5 mins)

Focus on some of the persuasive language used to support (and to counter) various groups' arguments, making use of language models the students have produced and adding any others you think would be useful. Modal verbs are a natural focus of this unit: 'we could', 'we would', etc. (5–10 mins)

Tourism – a good or bad thing?

Engage the students' interest in the topic – perhaps by asking them to suggest famous tourist places they have visited or would like to visit. Put some of the contributions on the board. Ask if the students think that tourism is generally good or bad for these places. (2–3 mins)

Instruct the students in pairs to prepare arguments for and against the statement that tourists destroy places of interest and should be kept out. Monitor, and prompt if you think the students need more ideas (eg, how can we keep tourists out/who is responsible for controlling tourists). (5 mins)

4   **People travel not just to get from one place to another, but also for interest and pleasure. In recent years, tourism has become more and more common. This can bring benefits to popular tourist destinations but it can also have negative effects.**
What arguments would you give for and against this statement: 'Tourists destroy places of interest and should be kept out'?
Here are one or two examples of arguments for and against.
Discuss them with your partner and add any more you can think of.

For	Against
'Tourists make places crowded and leave a lot of rubbish behind.'	'The money tourists bring can be used to improve places of interest.'

Elicit the students' contributions and put some of these on the board. You may need to reword some of the students' arguments for the purpose of presenting an accurate model of language. (5 mins)

Tell the students they are going to listen to two arguments (one for the statement, one against) and decide who wins. (2 mins)

Play the recording so that the students can check if the speakers put forward the ideas they suggested (and in the same words). (3–5 mins)

5   **Listen to two people arguing for and against the statement. Do they use the same arguments as you? If so, do they use the same words to express them?** 📼 61

📼 61
1

Male voice 'Tourism is out of control. There's nowhere in the world left unspoilt – I mean, everywhere you go you see crowds of people and piles of litter. If tourists just looked and took photographs, that would be all right, but they don't. They take away bits of ancient buildings – actual stones and other material; it's unbelievable! Another thing, tourists mean traffic and that's bound to ruin places of natural beauty: all that noise, pollution, and so on. Governments really must act now. A total ban on tourism is the only way to save the wonderful places we've got.'
2

Female voice 'There are so many advantages to tourism. For one thing, tourists bring money into places where it's needed. Tourists also make us keep old buildings and ancient monuments in good condition – if nobody was interested in them, they would probably be left to fall to pieces. And don't forget all the international understanding tourism encourages. I don't agree that we should control tourism and, in any case, I don't see how we could do it. And finally, what on earth is the point of having places of interest if nobody can visit them?'

Play the recording again and ask the students to discuss with a partner who wins the argument and why. They vote for the winner. (3–5 mins)

6 **Listen to the recording again. Discuss with a partner.**
   Who wins the argument and why?

This unit lends itself naturally to the use of certain modal verbs: 'must (not)'; 'should (not)'; 'ought (not) to'. The use of weak forms in producing, eg, 'shouldn't' is a useful study focus and there are several examples in the recording of the difference in emphasis between, eg, 'mustn't' and 'must not'. (5–10 mins)

3 College campus

Engage the students' interest in the topic by introducing the theme of college study, perhaps by using photos of a college campus, and telling them they're going to spend a year of study on a campus. (2–3 mins)

Congratulations! You have the opportunity to spend a year studying English at a college and you are going to live on the campus (see the plan below).

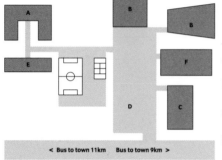

A   Student accommodation (built around 100 years ago)

B   Lecture halls (rather basic, not very comfortable)

C   Administration

D   Sports facilities (very limited)

E   Library (old-fashioned with no computers)

F   Dining hall (limited choice of food)

As you can see, the facilities are very basic. Unfortunately, the college is a little short of money and students have to go to town for most things. The good news is that the college has found a sponsor who is willing to pay for one new facility. The sponsor would like the students to argue the case for different new facilities and will decide which argument is the most convincing.

Ask the students individually or in pairs to say what facilities they would expect to find on a campus. Put some of the students' suggestions on the board. (5 mins)

Refer the students to the campus plan and the facilities listed. Explain what the terms mean, eg, 'Lecture Halls are places where students attend talks and presentations and take notes for their studies.' Present any vocabulary the students might need in connection with some of the facilities. (5 mins)

Explain that the students have the chance to persuade a sponsor to fund one facility by putting forward a convincing case. (3–5 mins)

Organise the students into groups and instruct them to prepare the case for their college campus facility. Make sure each group has a facility which is sufficiently different from the others to promote debate (eg, avoid gym and sports centre as separate choices – it is often best to draw lots to see which group gets which category or has the opportunity to choose their category first). Monitor while the students are preparing their arguments, and prompt where necessary. (10 mins)

1 **Some of the facilities students would like are listed below.
You and your partner are going to argue the case for one
of these facilities. Think of as many arguments as you can
and describe the facility you are suggesting.**

Facilities	Arguments	Description
More modern and comfortable student accommodation		
Sports centre		
Cinema		
Computer centre in the library		
Students' common room		
Better lecture halls and study rooms		
Other		

Choose the order in which the groups make their presentations – again,
it might be simplest to draw lots. Make sure that each group have their
full 2 minutes without interruption, prompting any group that seems
likely to dry up. At the end of each presentation, encourage the other
students to put questions and raise objections. If you need to give
groups of students the chance to expand on their presentation, you
can ask when the college students would use the facilities, what the
buildings would look like, etc. (3 mins per group)

2 **You have 2 minutes to argue your case and then the other pairs
or groups can ask questions for you to answer.**

Engage the students' interest in the next activity by explaining that they
are going to vote for the winners – the group which put forward the most
persuasive arguments for the facility. Recapitulate some of the main
points made by each group, correcting language where necessary.
(2–3 mins)

Instruct the students in their groups to discuss the arguments they have
heard. Monitor, and remind the students to say which arguments (not
necessarily the facilities they would like most in reality) persuaded them.
Ask the students to write their votes on a secret ballot paper and hand
them to you. (5–10 mins)

3 **Now discuss with your partner the arguments you heard.
Which were the best?
You are going to vote for the winners. (You can't vote for your own team!)**

Read out the votes and give the results. (3–5 mins)

Focus on some of the persuasive language used to support (and to counter) various groups' arguments, making use of language models the students have produced and adding any others you think would be useful. This unit lends itself naturally to a focus on conditional sentences, eg, 'If we build a sports centre, we'll all be fitter', 'If we bought more computers, we'd get better results in our studies.'
(5–10 mins)

Study – full-time or part-time?

Engage the students' interest in the theme of full-time and part-time study. Explain that they are going to hear arguments for both sides of the statement 'It's much better to study part-time than full-time.'
(2–3 mins)

4 Some people think it is more effective to study an intensive, full-time course at a college or university, while others think it's better to study part-time over a longer period. There are strong arguments on both sides. What arguments can you think of for and against this statement: 'It's much better to study part-time than full-time'?
Here are two examples. Discuss them with your partner and add any more you can think of.

For	Against
'You can earn money while you study.'	'You can't concentrate on your studies.'

Instruct the students in pairs to think of likely arguments to be put forward for and against the statement. Monitor, and prompt if the students are short of ideas. (5 mins)

Ask the students to contribute their ideas for arguments for and against the statements. Put some of these on the board. (2 mins)

Look at some of the ideas on the board and pick up on any language points which may give the students difficulties because of inaccuracies or lack of range. (5–10 mins)

Play the recording to allow the students to check if the arguments they suggested are included by the speakers and to decide which speaker won the argument. (5 mins)

5 **Listen to two people arguing for and against the statement, and decide who wins and why.** 📼 62

📼 62

1

Female voice 'I'm convinced that part-time study is better than full-time. In my opinion, and in my experience, you can learn much more effectively if you spread your studies over a longer period. You can also earn while you learn, and that's very important. Of course, you need a lot of self-discipline – nobody sets your timetable for you, you have to do it yourself. To be honest, I'd never be able to focus on any subject if I studied full-time. Having a life outside college provides me with the right balance; I mean, when I get home from work, I actually want to get down to my studies. If I studied full-time, I'm sure it would become boring, tedious – you know, a chore.'

2

Male voice 'Full-time! No doubt! You can't do things by halves, especially something as important as study. I know myself, and I know that if I tried to study part-time I'd lose concentration, be distracted by work, by family life and so on. And quite apart from the study itself, think of college life – you're part of something, you get involved in social life, sports, everything. At the moment, I'm in my third and final year of a degree course and I could never have completed it part-time. If you study full-time, you've also got the encouragement of fellow students: if you're tempted to drop out, your friends persuade you to go on.'

The language of obligation ('have to'/'don't have to'; 'can'/'can't') is a natural feature of the recording in this unit and is a useful study focus. (5–10 mins)

4 That's my story!

Engage the students' interest in the activity. One way is to tell a short story about yourself and make it so full of factual errors that the students will readily recognise that it is untrue. Another way is to tell them three 'facts' about yourself, only one of which is true, and get the students to guess which is true and which are invented.

Tell the students they are going to hear three people make the same claim, 'I used to be a full-time, professional artist'. (2–3 mins)

1   **You are going to hear three people talking. Each of them makes the same claim, tells their story and answers one or two questions.
The claim is: 'I used to be a full-time, professional artist.'
Only one of the three people is telling the truth, neither of the others has ever worked as an artist. Listen to the three people tell their story.** 📼 63

📼 63

1

Male voice 1 'I used to be a full-time professional artist. It all started when, just for fun, I drew pictures of friends, you know, portraits. They showed them to other people and they asked me to draw them too. After a couple of months I was producing 20 or 30 pictures a week and charging about £50 each – I gave up my job and concentrated on the art. Soon, I had hundreds of people asking me to draw their picture – it got out of hand, I just couldn't keep up with the demand. So I decided, "No, give it up." So I did.'

2

Female voice 'I used to be a full-time professional artist. I followed the traditional route – I went to art school and specialised in oil painting. My favourite style was Impressionist: Renoir, Monet, Pissaro. I don't claim I was as good as them, but I wasn't bad, and after I left college I got a job in a bookshop and kept up the painting in my spare time. I gave a few exhibitions and managed to sell a few works. Friends persuaded me to turn professional. I wasn't sure, but I gave it a go. I rented a studio down by the coast in Cornwall and painted full time for almost three years, but to be honest there just wasn't enough money in it – not enough to live on – so reluctantly I gave up and went into English language teaching. I still do a bit of painting in my spare time and sell the occasional work.'

3

Male voice 2 'I used to be a full-time professional artist. After I left school, I went to Italy for a year and I went round all the art galleries and took photos of the paintings by great Italian artists, like Leonardo da Vinci and Michelangelo. At home I copied the photos – it wasn't too difficult – and sold the paintings. It was so successful that I quickly made serious money: enough to retire after 18 months in fact.'

Ask the students in pairs to discuss what questions they would ask the speakers based on what they heard (play the recording a second time if you think appropriate). (5–10 mins)

2   **Talk with a partner. Which of the speakers do you think really was a professional artist? What makes you believe him or her?**

Tell the students they are going to hear the three speakers respond
to questions, which may help them decide who's telling the truth.
(2–3 mins)

Ask the student pairs to tell you what questions they would ask.
Put examples on the board. (5 mins)

Focus on ways in which questions can be put, eg, 'Can you tell me
more about…', 'I'd like to ask you about…' (5–10 mins)
Play the second part of the recording.

**3   What questions would you ask each of the people? Listen to the
next recording.** 🔊 64

🔊 64

**Female voice 2 'Thank you for all your stories. Now I've got one or two
questions I'd like to ask. Speaker number 1, you said around 20 or 30
pictures a week – surely that's impossible?'**

M1 'Not impossible, just very, very difficult to keep going. That's why I gave up.'

M3 'Speaker number 2, who paid for the exhibitions?'

**F1 'They didn't actually cost anything. A local school let me use their main
hall for free at the weekend.'**

F2 'Number 3; you said you took photographs of paintings, didn't you?'

M2 'Yes, that's right.'

F2 'But surely you can't take photos in an art gallery!?'

M2 'Yes, you can. You need a licence and you can't use flash – you need a special long
exposure lens in your camera – if you have those things, then it's not a problem.'

M3 'But number 3, it must be against the law to copy famous paintings?'

M2 'Not at all. You can't sell them as original paintings, of course, but you can copy them
and sign your own name.'

**F2 'Number 2, you said you couldn't make enough money painting. How did
you live for those three years?'**

F1 'I worked as a waitress in local hotels and cafés during the holiday season.'

M3 'Number 1. Have you stopped painting completely or do you ever paint pictures
these days?'

M1 'I'll paint if someone wants a portrait for a special occasion and is willing to pay the
right price, but otherwise, no.'

F2 'Number 3. Which other Italian artists did you copy?'

M2 (hesitates) '… er … I'm not very good with names, I just copy the paintings. Picasso,
was he Italian?'

**F2 'Thank you. Speaker number 2, what advice would you give to a young artist
who was thinking of becoming a full-time professional?'**

F1 'Keep painting, but don't give up the day job.'

M3 'Number 3, same question?'

M2 'Take the money and run.'

F2 'And number 1; your advice?'

M1 'Learn to paint fast.'

Allow the students to check if their questions are similar to those put
by the interviewer. (5 mins)

4   **Are these the same as the questions you suggested? Do you still think that your chosen speaker is the artist? Discuss with your partner.**

Tell the students it is their chance to vote for the speaker who really was a professional artist. (2–3 mins)

Ask the students in pairs to discuss and decide. Each pair/group has to give a joint vote so you may need to monitor to encourage language of persuasion and to prompt the students by reminding them of some of the claims made by the speakers. (5 mins)

Ask the students to record their votes – and to say where there were differences of opinion and how one of the pair managed to persuade his or her partner. (2–3 mins)

Play the third part of the recording, which gives the answer. (2 mins)

5   **Now listen to the recording to find out who is the real artist. Are you right? Did others in your class get the answer right?** 📼 65

📼 65

F2 'Right. We've discussed your stories, but we don't agree, do we?'

M3 'No, we don't. I think I know who it is. Number 1, you sounded very convincing. You may just be good at telling stories, but I think you were the artist.'

M1 'You're absolutely right … (pauses) I'm just good at telling stories. I've never been an artist, sorry.'

F2 'Good. So, I have a 50–50 chance. Number 2, you sounded very natural – the right art school background and all that … it must be you (slight pause) and yet, I can't stop thinking that number 3 might just be the one. It sounds so simple, just take photos and paint – even though you obviously don't know very much about artists! It sounds too good to be true, but I think it's you, number 3.'

M2 'You're right! … (pauses) it's much too good to be true. I've never even been to an art gallery – sorry.'

M3 'So, number 2, it was you.'

F1 'Yes. I used to be a full-time professional artist.'

F2 'Tell us all about it.'

F1 'Well, as I said, I went to art school and … ' *(fades)*

This is my story!

Tell the students it is now their turn to play the 'This is my story!' game. (2–3 mins)

Organise the students into groups of three or four. They are going to follow the 'professional artist' example and come up with a claim for a story that is true for one of them only. You may need to consider practical matters: reorganising furniture or using extra rooms to allow the students to plan without others overhearing. Monitor to ensure that the students are following the rules of the game and that everyone is taking part in the preparation – stress that the story doesn't need to be spectacular, the presentation is what matters. (10–15 mins)

6   Work with two or three partners. Talk together and find a story
     that is true for one of you.
     (Make sure the rest of the class don't know your story.)
     The story may be anything – funny, strange, unusual – but it must
     be true for one of your team. These are possible ideas:

A famous person you met or saw

A place you visited

An accident you had

A competition you won

Other

Set up the 'This is my story!' game. (Ideally, all groups of students will
be prepared to deliver a set of stories. If any group has not been able
to come up with anything, however, the students can still participate
by asking questions and putting counter-arguments.) (2–3 mins)

7   Plan together for a few minutes, then tell your story to the rest
     of the class. You have about 1 minute to speak, then the rest of
     the class can ask you any questions.
     Will they be able to guess which of you is telling the true story?

Timings will vary according to the number of students in the class but
the debate should take approximately 5 minutes for each group. It may
be best to allow more confident groups to tell their story first to give
their classmates a model. Make sure that each of the students in a group
has up to a minute and that the other groups save questions to the end.
If the other groups do not have questions for one of the students, join
in to give everyone the opportunity to respond. (5 mins per group)

At the end of each group's presentation and response to questions,
the other groups discuss what they have heard and, as a team, say
who they thought was telling the true story. (2 mins)

Instruct the students to discuss the story they've heard. Appoint a
spokesperson for each group. Ask each spokesperson to give the
decision of their group. (1–2 mins per story)

The winners are the group who fooled most of their classmates
and/or the group who spotted most of the fabricated stories.

This unit lends itself naturally to a focus on reported speech.
('I don't think it was x because he said he had never been in
hospital.') (5–10 mins)

5 Famous people

Engage the students' interest in the topic. One way of doing this is to use photos of people the students are likely to know. Another way is to use the game of '20 Questions'. (You choose a famous person, the students can ask any questions to find out his or her identity but you can only answer 'yes' or 'no' and the students are allowed up to 20 questions to find out who your famous person is.) (2–3 mins)

Ask the students in pairs or groups to discuss the types of people who become famous. Monitor to help students with any vocabulary they may lack. Take suggestions from the group and put several of these on the board. (5 mins)

Look at the categories of famous people in activity 1 and explain any items which may be unfamiliar. Focus on what it is that these people do to make them famous. (5 mins)

Set the scene for activity 1 by telling the students that they are going to invite a famous person to come and meet their class. The students will have the chance to meet the person and to ask him or her any questions they wish (for the same exercise we can introduce an interpreter if the famous person is not an English speaker!). The students in pairs or groups are going to argue the case for one famous person to be invited (no limits to the imagination, any living person is available). (5 mins)

Organise the students into groups and instruct them to argue the case for their category of person. Make sure each group has a different person (it is often best to draw lots to see which group gets which category or has the opportunity to choose their category first). Monitor while the students are preparing their arguments, and prompt where necessary. (10 mins)

1   **You and your partner are going to argue the case for inviting a famous person from the list below to meet your class and answer your questions. Talk together and decide which person you will invite. Make some notes below about the type of person you would choose.**

Type of person	Who?	Description
Pop star		
Politician		
Artist		
TV personality		
Writer		
Sports person		
Scientist		
Other		

Timings will vary according to the number of students in the class but the debate should take approximately three minutes for each group. Choose the order in which the groups make their presentations – again, it might be simplest to draw lots. Make sure that groups have their full 2 minutes without interruption, prompting any group that seems likely to dry up. At the end of each presentation, encourage the other students to put questions and raise objections. Whether or not people are expressing their true feelings is not the issue, the important thing is to keep the debate going; ideally the teacher will have no more than a referee's role, but should be ready to intervene if necessary. (3 mins per group)

2   **Now you have 2 minutes to present the case for the person you suggest inviting. Describe the person and say why you think it would be interesting for your class to meet him or her.**
Say what question(s) you would like to ask the famous person.
When you have given your arguments, the other students will have 1 minute to ask you questions.

Explain that the students are going to vote for the winners – the group which put forward the most persuasive arguments, whoever their famous person was. Recapitulate some of the main points made by each group, correcting language where necessary. (2–3 mins)

Instruct the students in their groups to discuss the arguments they have heard. Monitor, and remind the students to say which arguments impressed them. Ask the students to write their votes on a secret ballot paper and hand them to you. (5–10 mins)

3   Now you are going to vote for the winning group.
    Talk with your partner(s) about the arguments you heard and give
    3 points for the best argument, 2 points for the next best and 1 point
    for the third best. (Sorry, you can't vote for your own group!)

Read out the votes and give the results. (3–5 mins)

Focus on some of the persuasive language used to support (and to
counter) various groups' arguments, making use of the language models
the students have produced and adding any others you think would be
useful. (5–10 mins)

Fame and fortune – a dream or a nightmare?

Introduce the theme of fame and fortune as a mixed blessing. You might
like to ask if students know anyone famous (or can think of anyone
famous) and if they think that person is really happy. (2–3 mins)

4   Many people dream of being rich and famous; for others the idea
    is awful. What reasons can you think of why fame and fortune might
    be considered a dream or a nightmare? Here are some examples.
    Add any more you can think of and compare notes with a partner
    to see if you thought of similar arguments.

A dream	A nightmare
'Everyone wants to know you!'	'Nobody leaves you alone even for a minute.'
'You have so much money you never need worry.'	'You worry because you have too much money.'

Focus on the reasons the students have given and look at how the use
of linking devices such as 'because', 'although', 'on the one hand' can
help put an argument together. (5–10 mins)

Engage the students' interest in listening to the recording by telling
them they are going to hear two people arguing that fame and fortune
are either a dream or a nightmare. At the end, the students in the class
will vote to decide who presented the more persuasive case. (2–3 mins)

Instruct the students to listen to the recording. Play the recording a
second time if you think it will help the students decide who 'wins'.
(5 mins)

5   Now listen to two people arguing opposite cases: one that fame and fortune is a dream, the other that it is a nightmare. 📼 66

📼 66

1

Female voice   'Fame – that's my dream. I'd love to walk down the street and be recognised by everyone. Just imagine seeing your face on the front of every magazine and newspaper and having people come up to you in restaurants to ask for your autograph. I would give anything to be famous – even if it was only for a year – I'd love the glamour of a movie-star lifestyle. When I think of famous pop stars, sports people, celebrities and so on, I'm green with envy.'

2

Male voice   'Fame – what a nightmare. You'd never be able to go anywhere or do anything without people interrupting you and pestering you all the time. And just think of all the attention you'd get from the media, the photos they'd take everywhere you went. You'd have absolutely no privacy. Fame destroys all those who have it and, quite frankly, I wouldn't be able to cope with it. I'm happy to be myself, and if you're famous, you belong to the public.'

Instruct the students, in their groups, to discuss the arguments they have heard on the recording and to decide which speaker puts forward the better case – it isn't necessary for the students to reach a joint decision, but prompt them to quote the arguments which made them reach their decision. Take a vote on which argument wins. (5–10 mins)

6   Discuss with a partner the two arguments you have heard.
Do you agree on the winner or do you have different opinions?
What persuaded you?

Play the recording again and focus on some of the effective linguistic devices (including tone, stress and rhetorical features) used by the speakers in putting forward their case. (5–10 mins)

6 Time capsule

Engage the students' interest by setting the scene of the present being projected into the future (perhaps by showing a picture from a science-fiction film/programme). Explain the concept of the time capsule. (3–5 mins)

Ask the students in pairs to discuss the everyday objects we are so familiar with and to suggest which may disappear in our own lifetime and for what reasons. (5 mins)

Refer the students to the categories listed for activity 1. They can also add any of the suggestions on the board. Present any vocabulary you think the students may need to help describe any of the examples in the several categories. (5 mins)

Explain that in groups the students are going to argue for one of these examples as the object which will best show people in the future what life is like now. The debate allows for three items to be included. (2–3 mins)

Organise the students into groups and instruct them to prepare the case for their object to put in the time capsule. Make sure each group has a different type of object so that the arguments will be sufficiently different. (It is often best to draw lots to see which group gets which category or has the opportunity to choose their category first). Monitor while the students are preparing their arguments, and prompt where necessary. (10 mins)

1 A time capsule is a sealed box which contains everyday objects.
   It may be buried or sent into space for people in the future to find
   and open. The idea is to give people of the future a snapshot of our
   everyday lives.
   You and your partner are going to argue the case for an object
   that would best show people in the future what life is like today.
   Decide what example you will choose in your category.
   Describe the object, say what people use it for and say why it is
   such a typical part of life at the beginning of the 21st century.

Category	Example	Description
Something to read		
A child's toy		
Something to wear		
Something used in sport		
Something connected with travel		
Something to eat or drink		
A music cassette or CD		
Other		

Choose the order in which the groups make their presentations – again,
it might be simplest to draw lots. Make sure that each group have their
full 2 minutes without interruption, prompting any group that seems
likely to dry up. At the end of each presentation, encourage the other
students to put questions and raise objections. If the other groups are
not forthcoming in the question-and-answer phase, you could expand
the debate by asking the students to say what the object may make
people in the future think we used to do in our time. (3 mins per group)

2 You have 2 minutes to argue your case. Then the other pairs or groups
   can ask you questions.

Engage the students' interest in the next activity by explaining that they
are going to vote for the winners – the group which puts forward the
most persuasive arguments for an object to include in a time capsule
sent into the future. Recapitulate some of the main points made by each
group, giving a corrected version of the actual language used where
necessary. (2–3 mins)

Instruct the students in their groups to discuss the arguments they have heard. Monitor, and remind the students to say which arguments have most impressed them. Ask the students to write their votes on a secret ballot paper and hand them in to you. Give the students the chance to vote for the three best arguments. (5–10 mins)

3   **Discuss with your partner which group made the best arguments for their objects to go in the time capsule.**
(You can vote for three of the other groups, but not your own.)

Read out the votes and give the results – there will be three winning teams. (3–5 mins)

Focus on some of the persuasive language used to support (and to counter) various groups' arguments, making use of language models the students have produced and adding any others you think would be useful. Structures with 'used to' are a natural focus of this unit, eg, 'People will think we used to wear strange clothes/eat horrible things', etc. (5–10 mins)

It was the best of times, it was the worst of times

Engage the students' interest in the topic by asking them to think of the time we live in and give ideas of what is good and bad about it. (2–3 mins)

Ask the students in pairs to note down as many examples as they can think of to support the arguments that the time we live in is either especially good or especially bad. (5 mins)

4   **People at almost all times in history see the period they live in as special and unique. In what ways do you think the times we are living in now are especially good or bad? Make some notes below and compare your ideas with a partner.**

Best of times	Worst of times

Ask the students to contribute their arguments for the 'best of times, worse of times' debate and put some of these on the board. Focus on the language of explanation and description. (5–10 mins)

Engage the students' interest in listening to the recording by telling them they are going to hear two people putting forward opposing cases and that you are going to check if the speakers use any of the same arguments as the students. (2–3 mins)

Play the recording to allow the students to check if the arguments they thought of are used by the speakers. (5 mins)

5   Listen to two people talking about how they think people in the future will look back on our time. Which of them do you think gives the best arguments? ⏚ 67

⏚ 67

1

Male voice 'In my opinion, we are lucky enough to be living in a golden age and if we don't appreciate it, people in the future surely will. For the first time in history, we are able to provide for all our basic needs and we can control the temperature of the places we live and work in. These days, we can travel all over the world quickly and inexpensively – we can even travel into space. It's fantastic! And just think of all the advances in medical care. We have machines to save us all the hard, boring physical work people had to do only a few years ago. We see TV pictures of events as they happen and we can get to know and understand people from all the countries around the world.'

2

Female voice 'We could, and should, be living in wonderful times, but look around you and you'll see that we're not. Half the world has too much food, the other half hasn't got enough. We could improve our surroundings, but what do we do? We build huge cities and fill them with heavy traffic. We pollute the atmosphere and destroy nature. We waste billions going into space when there is so much here on earth that needs our attention. Do you know what people in the future will say about us? "They had it all, but they threw it all away."'

Focus on any different ways the same arguments were expressed. (5–10 mins)

Play the tape a second time if you think it helpful and ask the students to discuss in pairs who 'wins' the argument. Vote for the winner. (5 mins)

This unit lends itself naturally to a focus on future forms, including passives: 'People will think…', 'Our time is going to be remembered…', 'This year will be thought of…' (10 mins)

7 What a way to spend the weekend!

Engage the students' interest in the topic by asking if they have ever wished for more time to spend on one particular thing: playing sport, reading, watching films, etc. (2–3 mins)

Tell the students they are going to hear a recording of someone talking about a time when he was accidentally locked in a public library alone for an entire weekend. Before the students listen, they are going to discuss how they think he felt about this unusual situation. (2–3 mins)

Ask the students to look at the words in the list and to group these into positive and negative feelings – they may know some words and not others; don't teach them at this stage, the recording will give clues to meaning. (5 mins)

1   **You are going to hear someone talking about a time when he was accidentally locked in a public library.**
He uses some of the following words to describe his feelings.
Put a tick (✓) to say if the words express positive feelings and a cross (✗) for negative feelings.
Do you think the speaker will use more positive or negative words?

nervous ✗	excited ✓	anxious ✗	horrified ✗
relieved ✓	delighted ✓	uneasy ✗	pleased ✓
appalled ✗	worried ✗	amused ✓	thrilled ✓

Ask the students in pairs to discuss whether the speaker will use more positive or negative words to describe his feelings about this situation. (5 mins)

Play the tape to allow students to check if they were right about which words the speaker would use and if they had them in the correct positive or negative group. (5 mins)

2   **Listen to the recording.**
Did the way he said the words tell you if they describe negative or positive feelings? 📼 68

▭ 68

Male voice 'Looking back, I'm quite amused, actually, but that's not how I felt at the time.

'I was in a quiet corner of the library, lost in a travel book, and I lost all track of time. If they announced that the library was closing, I didn't hear it. It was quiet, but so it would be, I mean, it was a library. Then suddenly the lights went out and the quiet turned into complete silence.

'It didn't really register at first, and then I realised it was 6.30 on Friday evening, closing time. I was a bit worried so I went to the exit, but it was locked and there was no one around. The desk was empty, the shutters were down. I was locked in.

'I wasn't all that anxious really. I'd got my shopping, so I wasn't going to starve. The library was warm enough and there was a bathroom. "Oh well," I thought, "it looks like I'm here until tomorrow morning."

'Then I thought, "Hang on, tomorrow's Saturday, the library's closed – and all day Sunday too. I'm stuck here until Monday morning!" I was appalled, horrified. It wasn't the end of the world because I lived alone in those days, so no-one was going to worry that I hadn't come home, but the prospect of a whole lost weekend was terrible.

'There was no telephone I could use, the windows were all locked, I didn't see any way of attracting attention. So I settled down to read – what else was there to do? It was still light outside even though all the electric lights were turned off automatically.

'When it got dark I felt a little uneasy, the place was so quiet and empty, but I lay down on the floor and fell asleep. I was relieved when it got light. I had a little breakfast and settled down to read. I'd never had so much time to myself and I read all sorts of fascinating things and thought that, after all, a library wasn't the worst place to be locked in for the weekend.

'But I'll be honest – it didn't really come to that. Late on Saturday afternoon, I was absorbed in an encyclopedia when I heard the door open and in walked the cleaner! He was surprised to see me and I've never been so pleased to see anyone in all my life!'

Play the tape again and focus on the words used by the speaker. Pay attention to the way he uses phonological features to indicate positive (rising tone) and negative (falling tone) feelings and how the modifiers 'quite' and 'absolutely' add emphasis to the meaning. (5–10 mins)

The speaker told of a weekend spent (quite pleasantly) in a library. Ask the students to contribute ideas of better places to be stuck with time on your hands. Put some of these on the board. (2–3 mins)

Organise the students into groups and instruct them to argue the case for their place as the best to spend time. Make sure each group has a place sufficiently different from the others to make the arguments varied from group to group (it is often best to draw lots to see which group gets which category or has the opportunity to choose their category first). Monitor while the students are preparing their arguments, and prompt where necessary. (10 mins)

3 **The speaker's conclusion is that there are worse places to be locked in for a weekend – are there better places?**
You are going to choose and argue for the best place to have to spend a weekend. You have food and all the comforts you need, you are free to use anything you want and you can take one thing away when you leave! Here are some possible places:

sports shop

video games centre

clothes shop

swimming pool/fitness centre

art gallery

video shop

other

4 **Work with a partner to plan how you would spend the time.**

Choose the order in which the groups make their presentations – again, it might be simplest to draw lots. Make sure that each group have their full 2 minutes without interruption, prompting any group that seems likely to dry up. At the end of each presentation, encourage the other students to put questions and raise objections to the arguments put forward by their classmates (eg, why it might become tiring or tedious to spend so long on one type of activity). (3 mins per group)

5 **You have 2 minutes to describe the place you would be in and say how you would use the things in it.**
The other pairs or groups can then ask you questions.

Engage the students' interest in the next activity by explaining that they are going to vote for the winners – the group which put forward the most persuasive arguments for the best place to be stuck for the weekend. Recapitulate some of the main points made by each group, giving a corrected version of the language used. (2–3 mins)

Instruct the students in their groups to discuss the arguments they have heard. Monitor, and remind the students to say what arguments and descriptions of the places impressed them. Ask the students to write their votes on a secret ballot paper and hand them to you. (5–10 mins)

6 **Now discuss with a partner the arguments you heard.**
Which were the best ones? Vote for the best three.

Read out the votes and give the results. (5 mins)

Focus on some of the persuasive language used to support (and to counter) various groups' arguments, making use of language models the students have produced and adding any others you think will be useful. Speculating about what you could do is a natural focus of this unit, together with sequencing events. ('First you could…', 'After that you might want to…', 'Later you would probably…') (5–10 mins)

A lot of one or a little of many?

Engage the students' interest in the topic by asking these questions: 'Who plays several sports/plays only one sport a lot?' 'Who listens to all sorts of music/collects everything by one recording artist?' (Refer back to 'What a way to spend the weekend!' where people had time for just one thing.) (2–3 mins)

Instruct the students in pairs to think of as many arguments as they can for and against the statement (which you can write on the board): 'It is better to be an expert in one field than to know a little about a lot of things.' (5 mins)

7   Is it better to know as much as possible about one subject or play one sport as well as you can, or is it better to try a little of lots of things? Think of as many arguments as you can for and against the statement: 'It is better to be an expert in one field than to know a little about a lot of things.' Make notes.

For	Against
'If you go deeper into a subject, you get more out of it.'	'Life is too short to limit yourself to just one thing.'

Elicit the students' contributions. Put some of these on the board and focus on the language of explanation and comparison. (5–10 mins)

Tell the students they are going to listen to the recording to check if their arguments were also used by the speakers and to decide who 'wins' the debate. (2 mins)

Play the recording. Allow the students to check which of their arguments the speakers used. (3 mins)

8   Listen to the recording.
Did the speakers use the same arguments as you? 🔊 69

📼 69

1

Female voice 'If I do something, I want to do it as well as I possibly can, and that means focusing on it completely. If I study, I want to study one subject in detail, in depth, not learn little bits about all sorts of different things. If I play a sport, I don't want to waste my time playing others badly; I want to improve my skills in the sport I'm best at. And as for work, surely it's obvious that you need to find out what you can do and do it to the best of your ability. I want to be an expert, a specialist, a professional, not just do things in a half-hearted way.'

2

Male voice 'When I was at school, they made us choose a limited number of subjects and learn far more about them than we actually needed to know. I wanted to do everything – physics, chemistry, geography. But instead, from my mid-teens, I was forced to read so much about history that I've come to hate the subject. I think that's why these days I like to try my hand at different things. I would hate the idea of having just one job all my life; I need the change, the chance to try new things constantly. And I can't understand how anyone can bear to spend all their time on just one hobby or sport. That would drive me mad. Variety is the spice of life, after all.'

Instruct the students in pairs to discuss which of the speakers put forward the most persuasive arguments and what made their presentation particularly effective. Play the recording a second time. (5 mins)

---

9   **Listen again and discuss what you hear with a partner.**
      Which of the speakers do you think wins the debate?

Vote on the 'winner'. (2–3 mins)

This unit lends itself to a focus on conditional sentences with 'if' and 'unless', eg, 'If you spent all your time listening to one composer you'd miss so much wonderful music' and 'Unless you try something, you don't know if you're good at it'. (5–10 mins)

---

8 Modern technology

The topic of modern technology is a common one and is very easy to introduce and illustrate by using props or photos.

Introduce the activity of planning to argue a case for the most beneficial machine used in the home. You may need to explain some of the items on the list of household machines in activity 1 – the best way to do this is probably to let the students look at the list and tell you if there is anything unfamiliar there.

The debate will work best if each pair of students argues the case for a different item on the list – or one they add to the list – and then puts counter-arguments when the other pairs present their cases. One way to ensure that every pair has a different case to argue is to draw lots for the items in the list.

Ask the students, in pairs, to discuss together all the arguments they can think of to support their case. Monitor, and supply language and ideas if this is needed. (10 mins)

Then set up the debate. It is often a good idea to draw lots to decide which pair of students goes first, second, etc.

Ask the first pair of students to present their case. Make sure that none of the other students interrupts, but ask them to listen and make any notes if they wish (they'll shortly have the chance to give counter-arguments). Note any particularly effective use of language to argue a case. (2 mins per group)

1   These days, most people's lives are very strongly influenced by things that were invented or developed in the last hundred years. You and your partner are going to choose and argue the case for one of these (or another) as 'the most beneficial machine used in the home'. Work with your partner to think of as many arguments as you can for the invention you are supporting. You have 2 minutes to argue your case. Then the other pairs or groups can ask you questions.

vacuum cleaner

washing machine

refrigerator

toaster

microwave oven

dishwasher

coffee maker

Now ask the rest of the class, in a free-for-all, to raise as many queries and give as many arguments as they can to put the opposite case. Without appearing to take sides, you may like to contribute by asking the original pair of candidates to explain and justify some of their arguments. (5 mins)

Repeat the procedure to give every pair of students the chance to argue their case. (Timings will vary according to student numbers. With very large classes you may wish to have groups rather than pairs. The important thing is that everyone gets into the habit of thinking about what they want to say and gets as much opportunity as possible to take an extended turn and respond to follow-up prompts.)

When everyone has argued their case, organise the process of deciding which argument wins (who used language most persuasively to argue their case). One way to do this is to give each pair the chance to vote for the others (not themselves), giving 3 points to the best argument, 2 points for the next best and 1 point for the third best. Ask the student pairs to write down their votes and hand them to you. Put the running total on the board as you read out each vote. (Timings will vary.)

In a whole-group activity, discuss what it was about the most successful arguments which earned them the votes, drawing on any notes you made during the presentations. (5–10 mins)

Has modern technology improved our lives?

Now ask the students to think about the broader topic 'Has modern technology improved our lives?' Tell them they are going to hear arguments for and against and ask them in pairs to speculate about the arguments and statements they may hear. (5 mins)

In a whole-group activity, invite the students to tell you what arguments they and their partner think they are likely to hear. Put on the board some of the students' suggestions. (5 mins)

2 Many people argue that life was better before we had the modern technology which exists today. Others think that these inventions have improved our lives. What arguments can you think of for and against this statement:
'Life was better before we had the technology of the 20th century'?
Below are one or two ideas. Discuss them with your partner and add any more you can think of.

Life was better before	Life is better now
'People had time to do things.'	'We can do things quickly.'
'We were much more creative.'	'Machines can do everything for us.'

Play the recording and ask the students to note whether any of the things they expected to hear were used by the speakers. Ask them also to decide which of the speakers wins the argument and why (there is no 'right' or 'wrong' answer to this; the idea is to listen to and quote the effective use of language of argument.) (2 mins)

3   Listen to two people arguing for and against the statement and decide who wins and why. 🔲 70

🔲 70

1

Female voice 'I couldn't imagine a world without modern technology; in fact, I don't even want to think about it. My computer gone?! And my mobile phone?! What an awful thought! No microwave to save hours in the kitchen? No washing machine or dishwasher to do the jobs I hate? As far as I'm concerned, we should keep on developing technology as much as we possibly can. Progress is always a good thing and anyone who thinks otherwise is living in the past.'

2

Male voice 'We've gone too far. Modern technology is destroying the world we live in and the way we live in it. The computer has taken away the need for us to think and learn – it just does it all for us. The Internet is full of rubbish and people spend literally hours in front of a screen instead of actually doing something and being creative. All the labour-saving devices we have in the home simply stop us learning to do things for ourselves. I wonder how many people these days could actually make a fire or do any of the really useful things their grandparents could do. Sooner or later, we're going to have to say "enough, no more" and get rid of all the things we don't need.'

In a whole-group activity, ask the students to tell you which of the speakers they and their partner decided won the argument. Play the recording again, pausing to focus on any language items the students found effective in supporting the case argued. (5–10 mins)

Test practice

The organisation of the test practice is a matter for your judgement in the particular teaching situation you are in. With larger classes, it can be difficult to use the practice test as an activity in class time. You can ask the students to practise in pairs, with one adopting the role of interlocutor, but if it is possible to conduct the practice exercise (and at some stage a full practice test) yourself or have a fellow teacher do so, it will be valuable test preparation.

(This type of task would normally take only a few minutes in the test itself and one of the test skills to cultivate is a fluent exchange of information/comment in a short time.)

Test practice – Achiever

The following topic is similar to the one you will be asked to talk about in Part 4 of the Spoken ESOL test at Achiever level. You will be asked some follow-up questions after you have finished talking about your topic. The interlocutor will say:

'… in the last part of the test I want you to speak about … I'll also ask you some questions. You have a short time to think about what you want to say and make some notes if you wish. Then I'll tell you when to begin.'

Topic – Achiever
'A famous person I would like to meet.'

Follow up questions
'Would you like to be famous? Why/Why not?'

'What do you think is the worst thing about being famous?'

'What would you like to be famous for?'

'Do you think famous people are paid too much? Why/why not?'

Test practice – Communicator

The following topic is similar to the one you will be asked to talk about in Part 4 of the Spoken ESOL test at Communicator level. You will be asked some follow-up questions after you have finished talking about your topic. The interlocutor will say:

'… in the last part of the test I want you to speak about … I'll also ask you some questions. You have a short time to think about what you want to say and make some notes if you wish. Then I'll tell you when to begin.'

Topic – Communicator
'The influence that TV has upon the people who watch it.'

Follow up questions
'Which TV programmes do you dislike? Why?'

'How much TV do children watch in your country?'

'If you could appear on a TV programme, which one would it be?'

'How do you see TV developing over the next twenty years?'

Exam information

A description of the exam at Achiever and Communicator levels is given in the student book. You should review this with your students prior to the test, to make sure that the students understand the format the test will take. Explain to the students that they won't use an exam paper in the test. The interlocutor will give them different tasks to do. The activities in the student book are there to help them to prepare for the test at Achiever and Communicator level.

Sample interlocutor's scripts

In this book we have included two sample tests at Achiever and Communicator levels, for you to use to prepare students for the Spoken ESOL test. The sample tests enable you to see the differences between the two levels and to set a mock exam practice with your students. This type of practice can be invaluable in preparing students for the way the exam is structured. The Spoken ESOL test is a test of their speaking skills in English. The important thing is for them to practise speaking as much as they can, with you and with other students.

Exam information

The Spoken ESOL exam at the Achiever level

Introduction

The following description of the exam at Achiever level will give you a good idea of what to expect. You are advised to confirm with your teacher the exact time allocations that apply for the Achiever level when you are taking the exam.

Part 1

The interlocutor will begin by asking your name and the spelling of your surname. He/she will ask you where you are from and five more questions about yourself. They might be such questions as 'What do you like to do at the weekends?' or 'What's your idea of a healthy meal?'

Part 2

The interlocutor will give you four situations. In two of the situations you will need to reply to a question that the interlocutor asks you. For example, the interlocutor might say: 'I'm a new student in your English class. I start. "What's your teacher like?"' You would need to answer this question as though you were talking to a new student. In two of the situations you will need to start the conversation. For example, the interlocutor might say: 'I'm your manager. You feel ill. You want to go home. You start.' You would then ask if you could go home as though you were talking to your manager.

The dialogue in all cases should run to at least four turns, that is two for you and two for the interlocutor.

Part 3

You and the interlocutor will have a discussion in order to carry out a task. For example, the interlocutor might say: 'I want you to imagine that we're choosing a wedding present for a friend. We need to decide what would be best. Here are some ideas.' The interlocutor will show you a picture with various choices such as a flowers, money and cooking pots. You and the interlocutor ask and answer questions to decide which present to give.

Part 4

The interlocutor will ask you to talk about a topic. For example, he/she might say: 'Tell me about your most exciting experience'. You will have a short time to think. You will then talk on this topic. The interlocutor will then ask you a few questions. For example, he/she might ask: 'What other exciting things would you like to do?'

The Spoken ESOL exam at the Communicator level

Introduction

The following will give you a good idea of what to expect at the Communicator level. You are advised to confirm with your teacher the exact time allocations that apply for the Communicator level when you are taking the exam.

Part 1

Again, the interlocutor will begin by asking your name and the spelling of your surname. He/she will ask you where you are from and five more questions about yourself. They might be such questions as 'How has your home town changed since you were a child?' or 'Which newspapers and magazines do you regularly read and why?'

Part 2

The interlocutor will give you four situations. In two of the situations the interlocutor will speak first. For example, the interlocutor might say: 'I'm your neighbour. "I hate to complain, but the music coming from your flat is so loud."' You would need to reply as though you were talking to your neighbour.
In two of the situations you will need to start the conversation. For example, the interlocutor might say: 'We're classmates. You're having a party. Invite me and give me details.'
The dialogue in all cases should run to four turns, that is two for you and two for the interlocutor.

Part 3

You and the interlocutor will have a discussion in order to carry out a task. For example, the interlocutor might say: 'I want you to imagine that we're making plans to go to a music concert next week. Here is your diary and some music events that are playing all week. I have my diary and a list of different music events. Let's ask and answer questions to find a concert and a time that suits both of us.' You and the interlocutor would decide which concert to attend.

Part 4

The interlocutor will ask you to talk about a topic. For example, he/she might say: 'How could you improve the place where you study?' You will have a short time to think. You will then talk on this topic. The interlocutor will then ask you a few questions. For example, he/she might ask: 'Do you prefer to study alone or in a group?' 'Why?'

Sample interlocutor's script, Achiever level

Introduction to the teacher

The following sample interlocutor's script can be used for mock exams at the Achiever level. It may be useful for this practice to be recorded and for the students to hear themselves speaking on the tape, to help them to understand what areas of their pronunciation or vocabulary need further practice. It is important to note that the questions and topics listed here will vary from those given in the actual exam. You are advised to confirm with City & Guilds the exact time allocations that apply for each part of the exam. See www.cityandguilds.com/ieq.

Part 1

Interlocutor 'City & Guilds Qualifications Spoken ESOL Test, Achiever level.
Candidate (give candidate's name). Test begins.
Hello. My name's…. Can you spell your family name for me, please?'
Candidate (Candidate spells surname.)
I 'Thank you. And where are you from?'
C (Candidate replies.)
I 'Right. Now I'm going to ask you a few more questions.'
(Ask one question from each topic area.)

Work/School
'How do you get to work/school?'

'Tell me about your typical day at work/school.'

'What do you like best about your work/school?'

'What do you remember about your first day at work/school?'

Free time
'How much free time do you have in a week?'

'What do you like to do in your free time?'

'How do you usually spend the weekend?'

'What sports do you enjoy watching and what sports do you enjoy playing?'

Food
'What did you have for breakfast today?'

'What was your favourite food when you were a child? What didn't you like?'

'What are you going to have for dinner this evening?'

'What kind of food do you enjoy making?'

Travel

'What kinds of transport have you used?'

'Which kind of transport do you like best? Why?'

'What was the last journey you made? Can you tell me about it?'

'How often do you use public transport? What do you think of it?'

The Internet

'How often do you use the Internet?'

'What do you use the Internet for?'

'What do you think about computer games?'

'Do you prefer to phone, text or send emails to people? Why?'

C   **(Answers 5 questions.)**

Part 2

I **'Thank you. Now, Part 2. I'm going to read four situations and we're going to act out each of them. I'll tell you when to start or reply.'**

Choose two situations from A. Read each situation then enact it with the candidate. Each dialogue should run up to at least four turns. Start by saying: 'First situation …', 'Second situation …'.

A

'I'm your friend. I want to go to the cinema. I start. "Hi! How about going to see a film together this evening?"'

'I'm your English teacher. I want to give the class more homework. I start. "I think you should have more homework. Do you agree?"'

'I'm a stranger in your town. I start. "Excuse me. Can you tell me where the nearest railway station is, please?"'

'I'm a stranger. I knock over your drink in a café. I start. "Oh dear. I'm so sorry!"'

Now choose two situations from B. Read each situation then enact it with the candidate. Each dialogue should run up to at least four turns. Start by saying: 'Third situation …', 'Last situation …'.

B

'I'm your friend. You promised to help me mend my car. Now you can't come. You start.' (suggest another time)

'I'm an English Language School director. Tell me what kind of course you want. You start.' (ask about course level, dates, etc)

'I'm your friend. Invite me to come and stay with you this weekend. Suggest what we could do together. You start.'

Finish by saying:

I **'Thank you.'**

Part 3

I   'Let's move on to Part 3. In this part of the test we're going to discuss
     something together.
     'We have been invited to a wedding. We need to decide on a suitable
     present to give the bride and groom. Here are some ideas. (Hand over
     candidate's copy of the picture.) Let's ask and answer questions to help us
     make a decision. I'll start.'

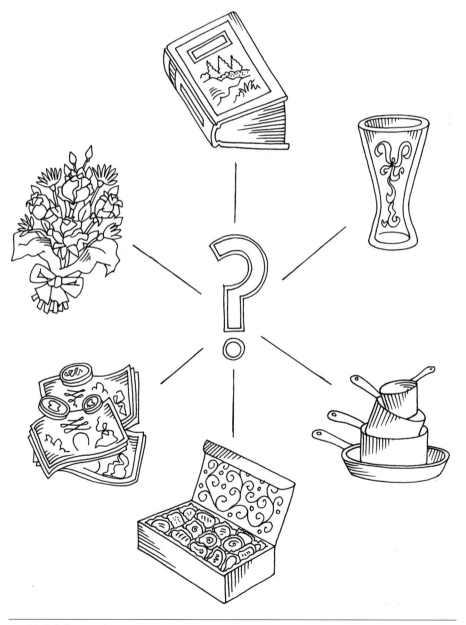

Finish by saying:

I   'Thank you.' (Retrieve candidate's copy of picture.)

Candidate's copy

Part 4

Choose one of the topics A, B or C below.

I **'Now Part 4. I want you to tell me about** (read out the topic you have chosen). **First you have a short time to think about what you want to say. You can make some notes if you like.**
(Hand over a piece of paper and pen/pencil.)
'Then I'll ask you to begin. I'll also ask you some questions. All right?'
(Withdraw eye contact.)

Topics

A 'My best friend'

B 'An exciting day in my life'

C 'How to keep fit'

I **'Ready? Please start.'**
C (Talks on topic, with support when appropriate.)
I (Ask a selection of follow-up questions, as appropriate.)

Follow up questions

A 'My best friend'
'How did you meet your friend?'

'Why are friends important?'

'What sorts of things do you do together?'

B 'An exciting day in my life'
'Would you like another day like this? Why/why not?'

'What other exciting things do you hope to do in the future?'

'Which films do you think are exciting?'

C 'How to keep fit'
'What kinds of food are good for your health?'

'How can schools help children to keep fit?'

'What things are bad for your health? Why?'

Finish by saying:

I **'Thank you. That is the end of the test for** (give candidate's name).**'**

Sample interlocutor's script, Communicator level

Introduction to the teacher

The following sample interlocutor's script can be used for mock exams at the Communicator level. It may be useful for this practice to be recorded and for the students to hear themselves speaking on the tape, to help them to understand what areas of their pronunciation or vocabulary need further practice. It is important to note that the questions and topics listed here will vary from those given in the actual exam. You are advised to confirm with City & Guilds the exact time allocations that apply for each part of the exam. See www.cityandguilds.com/ieq.

Part 1

Interlocutor 'City & Guilds Qualifications Spoken ESOL Test, Communicator level. Candidate (give candidate's name). Test begins.
Hello. My name's…. Can you spell your family name for me, please?'
Candidate (Candidate spells surname.)
I 'Thank you. And where are you from?'
C (Candidate replies.)
I 'Right. Now I'm going to ask you a few more questions.'
(Ask one question from each topic area.)

Home Life
'Do you live in a house or a flat? Tell me something about your home.'

'What kinds of things do you do with your family?'

'Tell me something about family meals.'

'Which member of your family are you most like? In what way?'

Work
'How do you/will you use English in your job?'

'What do you think would be the perfect job? Why?'

'Is there a job you wouldn't like to do? Why not?'

'Is the salary the most important thing for you? Why/why not?'

Music
'Which sort of music do you enjoy listening to?'

'What do you think about background music in shops and other public places?'

'Which musical instrument would you most like to play?'

'Which music do you dislike most? Why?'

The Environment

'Tell me something about the natural features in the area where you live.'

'What kinds of things do you recycle?'

'How can we improve the problem of litter?'

'Tell me about an outdoor area where you like to spend time.'

Sport

'How important is sport in your life?'

'Do you think sports people are paid too much? Why/Why not?'

'How much sport do you/did you play at school?'

'Which new sport would you like to learn? Why?'

C   (Answers 5 questions.)

Part 2

I   **'Thank you. Now, Part 2. I'm going to read four situations and we're going to act out each of them. I'll tell you when to start or reply.'**

Choose two situations from A. Read each situation then enact it with the candidate. Each dialogue should run up to at least four turns. Start by saying: 'First situation …', 'Second situation …'.

A

'I'm your friend. I start. "Hi! What're you doing this weekend?"'

'I'm your English teacher. I start. "Tell me what you find most difficult about learning English."'

'I'm your neighbour. I start. "I've run out of coffee. Could you lend me some, please?"'

'I'm a stranger in your town. I start. "Excuse me, where's the best place to eat around here?"'

Now choose two situations from B. Read each situation then enact it with the candidate. Each dialogue should run up to at least four turns. Start by saying: 'Third situation …', 'Last situation …'.

B

'You're in a hotel. I'm the manager. There's a problem with your room. Complain. You start.'

' You're in class. I'm the teacher. Explain why you have to leave early. You start.'

'You're in a bank. You want to change some money into British pounds. Ask. You start.'

'You've lost your bag. You're at the police station. Describe your bag and its contents. You start.'

Finish by saying:

I   **'Thank you.'**

Part 3

I 'Now let's move on to Part 3. In this part of the test we're going to ask and answer questions to exchange information and make some decisions.
(Hand over candidate's task sheet.)
'Our two families have decided to have a camping holiday together. Here is your weekly planner for June and July and some information about a camp-site. My weekly planner and camp-site details are different. Let's decide when to go. Take a short time to think about what you want to say. (Pause.)
'Why don't you start?'

(Make sure candidate answers and asks questions.)

Interlocutor's Weekly Planner
June

Week commencing 4th June	work
Week commencing 11th June	free
Week commencing 18th June	work
Week commencing 25th June	free

July

Week commencing 2nd July	work
Week commencing 9th July	free
Week commencing 16th July	free
Week commencing 23rd July	course/college

Sandy Bay camp site

50 metres from Sandy Bay Beach (safe swimming)

50 family tents & 30 caravans

Each site with own parking space

Children's playground

Café

Cost per week: £70 per person

Finish by saying:

I 'Thank you.' (Retrieve candidate's task sheet.)

Candidate's Weekly Planner

June

Week commencing 4th June	free
Week commencing 11th June	work
Week commencing 18th June	free
Week commencing 25th June	painting the house

July

Week commencing 2nd July	work
Week commencing 9th July	free
Week commencing 16th July	work
Week commencing 23rd July	free

Riverside camp site

By River Lyle – fishing, walking, horse-riding

150 deluxe tents & caravans (all with electricity)

Central car park (no parking next to tents)

Indoor swimming pool

Excellent restaurant

Cost per week: from £200 for 2 people to £600 for 8 people

Part 4

Choose one of the topics A, B or C below.

I 'Now Part 4. I want you to tell me about (read out the topic you have chosen). First you have a short time to think about what you want to say. You can make some notes if you like.
(Hand over a piece of paper and pen/pencil.)
'Then I'll ask you to begin. I'll also ask you some questions. All right?'
(Withdraw eye contact.)

Topics

A 'What you would change about TV programming in your country'

B 'An important day in your life'

C 'The best place for tourists to visit in your area'

I 'Ready? Please start.'
C (Talks on topic, with support when appropriate.)
I (Ask a selection of follow-up questions, as appropriate.)

Follow up questions

A 'What you would change about TV programming in your country'
'Should TV be educational or entertaining?'

'How much TV do you watch?'

'Does TV influence young children?'

'Do you prefer to watch films on TV or at the cinema? Why?'

B 'An important day in your life'
'How do you make sure you remember special occasions?'

'Why do some people keep diaries?'

'What kinds of things do you remember from your childhood?'

'What special days are you looking forward to?'

C 'The best place for tourists to visit in your area'
'What makes a place good for tourism?'

'Which places would you like to travel to?'

'Which is the best place you've ever visited? Why?'

'What effect do tourists have on the places they visit?'

Finish by saying:

I 'Thank you. That is the end of the test for (give candidate's name).'